MECHANIC AGRICULTURAL MACHINERY SECOND YEAR

OBJECTIVE QUESTION ANSWERS

MANOJ DOLE

Made with ♥ on the Notion Press Platform
www.notionpress.com

Digitization is the need of the time. In the future, training in industrial training institutes will need to be conducted using online internet to make training more convenient and easy. E-books containing a set of MCQ questions will be made available to the trainees as they need to be more accustomed to the multiple choice questions MCQ to prepare for the online exams taking place in their industrial training institutes.

With all these factors in mind, Mr. Manoj Madhukar Dole Instructor, Industrial Training Institute, Satara, has written books according to the new annual system and NSQF-5 syllabus. And they've created theoretical mobile apps and blogs to make training easier, and made all these educational materials available for download on the world famous websites Google Play Store, Amazon and Apple Book Store.

The books were published by Hon'ble Joint Director Shri Rajendra Ghume Saheb Regional Office of Vocational Education and Training, Pune on 9/1/2019, at this time Shri Prakash Saigavkar Saheb Principal Government Industrial Training Institute Aundh Pune, Shri Tukaram Misal Saheb Principal Govt. Q. Sanstha Satara, Shri Sachin Dhumal Saheb District Vocational Education and Training Officer Satara, Shri Yatin Pargaonkar Saheb Principal Govt. Q. Sanstha Kolhapur, Shri Vikas Teke Saheb Inspector Vocational Education and Training Regional Office Pune, Palekar Foods Products Pvt. Ltd. Entrepreneurial Chairman of Satara Mr. Nilkanthrao Palekar Saheb, Chairman of Hira Foods Mr. Ibrahim Baba Tamboli Saheb, Mrs. Shalmali Pawar Headmaster Government Technical School Center Satara and other dignitaries were present on the occasion.

Contents

Prologue

Mechanic Agricultural Machinery Second Yearis a simple e-Book for ITI Engineering Course Mechanic Agricultural Machinery, Revised NSQF Syllabus, It contains objective questions with underlined & bold correct answers MCQ covering all topics including all about the latest & Important about Mould Board Plough. disc Plough. tillage and its Implements. Record information of Tillage and its implementation system. Chisel Plough. Rotavator. rotavator operation. Disc harrows (Off set Type/Double action. and single action.). power harrows. harrows operation. Cultivators. cultivators systems. soil forming equipments. Lazar leveler, trencher & post hole digger. soil farming equipments. Dismantling & assembling of seed drills.. seed drills. planters. Fertilizer applicators. volute type centrifugal pump. Servicing of a submersible pump. Servicing of irrigation valves and hydrants. Servicing of Power tiller/power weeder. Cultivator. power tillers/ power weeder. grain handling seed treating and drying and check functionality of major components and assemblies of AC motors. AC motors. sprayers & dusters. sprayers & dusters. reaper, reaper winder, straw-reapers.reaper, reaper winder, straw-reapers. Thresher, Maize seller, Ground nut decorticator. Thresher, Maize seller, Ground nut decorticator. combine harvester- cutter bar assembly, feeder unit, threshing unit, separating unit. mower, folder harvester, power chaff/silage cutter. mower, folder harvester, power chaff/silage cutter. rotary harvester, hay bailer. groundnut digger, potato / onion digger. groundnut digger, hay bailer, potato / onion digger. Servicing of winnower, cleaner & grader. winnower, cleaner & grader. Servicing of rice huller, polisher, feed grinder-cum-mixer, hammer mill. rice huller, polisher, feed grinder-cum-mixer, hammer mill. grain handling seed treating and drying equipment and lots more.

We add new question answers with each new version. Please email us in case of any errors/omissions. This is arguably the largest and best e-Book for All engineering multiple choice questions and answers.

As a student you can use it for your exam prep. This e-Book is also useful for professors to refresh material.

Foreword

Vocational education and training is imparted through the Department of Vocational Edůcation and Training through the Department of Business Education and Business Practical to supply multi-skilled artisans in line with the rapidly growing demand in the industrial sector in the 21st century. All the occupations within the institutions are important, as the trainees from these occupations develop multi-skills as per the demands of the industry.

with the noble intention of making available MCQ e-books suitable for all businesses, considering that all the examinations in all the industries in the industrial sector are conducted online and include MCQ method questions. Mr. Manoj Madhukar Dole has written a very good e-book on MCQ method as per the new annual syllabus. This e-book will definitely be a guide for all the trainees, trainee candidates, training instructors and others concerned.

The author of the book is Mr. Manoj Madhukar Dole, Instructor Gov. ITI Satara has 17 years of training experience. Written as a new annual pattern, this e-book incorporates modern digital QR Code technology to understand the layout, simple language, and simple syntax, diagrams and videos for each subject. So I am sure that this e-book will definitely be useful for in-depth study and exam practice. The work they have done is certainly commendable.

Mr. Tukaram Misal
Principal Government Industrial Training Institute Satara.

Preface

DGET New Delhi and CSTARI Kolkata have been implementing an annual pattern for all businesses in ITI since the August 2018 session. The examination system will also be changed and it will be online from this year and since all the questions are of Objective Type (MCQ), the trainees are in dire need of in-depth study. It is with this in mind that we are delighted to present the books based on the old NIMI pattern and a complete overview of the new annual pattern, and we hope that these books will be a guide for all business directors and trainees. Is.

For writing these books, Johar Awate Saheb, Principal of ITI Akluj. Former Principal of ITI Satara Saigavkar Saheb, Assistant Director Shri Chandrakant Dhekne Saheb Regional Office of Vocational Education and Training, Pune, District Vocational Education and Training Officer Sachin Dhumal Saheb and Headmaster Government Technical School Kendra Shalmali Pawar Madam and son Adhiraj Dole, mother Kusum Dole, I am very grateful to my father Madhukar Dole and wife Ashwini Dole for their special guidance and cooperation from time to time.

Also, in a very short period of time, the book was reviewed by Shri Rajendra Ghume Saheb, Joint Director, Vocational Education and Training Regional Office, Pune, for his invaluable time in publishing the book. I am sincerely grateful for their feedback.

I am grateful to the Instructor of ITI Satara for there continuous support from the very beginning of writing the book.

From this book, I consider myself blessed to have shared my thoughts on e-learning with you. I will not claim that this book is perfect, because considering the perfection, this book is an attempt and is in its infancy. They will be valuable for improvement if they are tested and suggested.

Manoj Dole
Dated 9/1/2019

Acknowledgements

The industrial training and theoretical examination system of our industrial training institutes and these changes have been accepted by the craft instructors and the trainees. Theoretical examinations conducted in your industrial training institutes are also conducted online. Since these examinations are of multiple choice MCQ method, the trainees will need to get more practice of such questions.

With all these considerations in mind, Mr. Manoj Madhukar, Director, Dole Crafts, Katari Industrial Training Institute, Satara, has done a thorough study and with his diligent work and added his keen intellect, according to the new annual system and NSQF-5 syllabus, e-book of Katari and other machine trades. -Book) and they have created mobile apps and blogs on theoretical topics to make training easier and have made all these educational materials available for download on the world famous websites Google Play Store, Amazon and Apple Book Store. Training has been made easier by creating a print version and using advanced techniques like QR Code.

All these educational materials will definitely be a guide for all the trainees for in-depth study and for the craft instructors and other concerned who are imparting vocational training.

CHAPTER ONE

Mechanic Agricultural Machinery Second Year Drawings

Online Test Exam
ITI Books
CNC Course
AutoCAD CAM
JOB & Apprentice
Online Theory
Computer Course
Trading Course
Web Designing
MSCIT Course
Shopping Business
Internet Business
Remotasks Course
Online Services
Top Sportsmans
Indian Army
Freedom Fighters
Top Scientists
Social Reformers
Motivational Speaker
Top Richest People
Join WhatsApp Group
Join Facebook Group
Like Facebook Page
PAN / Adhar / Licence
Passport

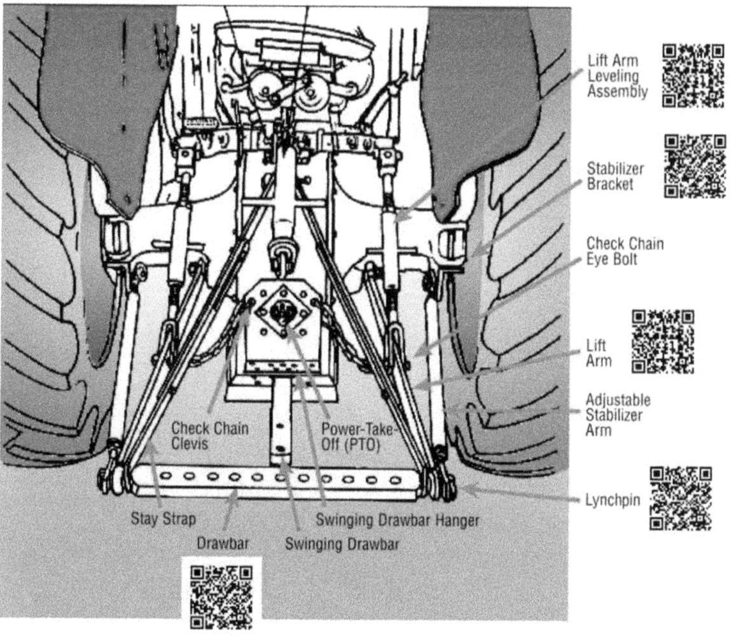
Lift Arm
Leveling
Assembly
Stabilizer
Bracket
Check Chain
Eye Bolt
Lift
Arm
Adjustable
Stabilizer
Arm
Lynchpin
Check Chain
Clevis
Power-Take-
Off (PTO)
Stay Strap
Swinging Drawbar Hanger
Drawbar
Swinging Drawbar

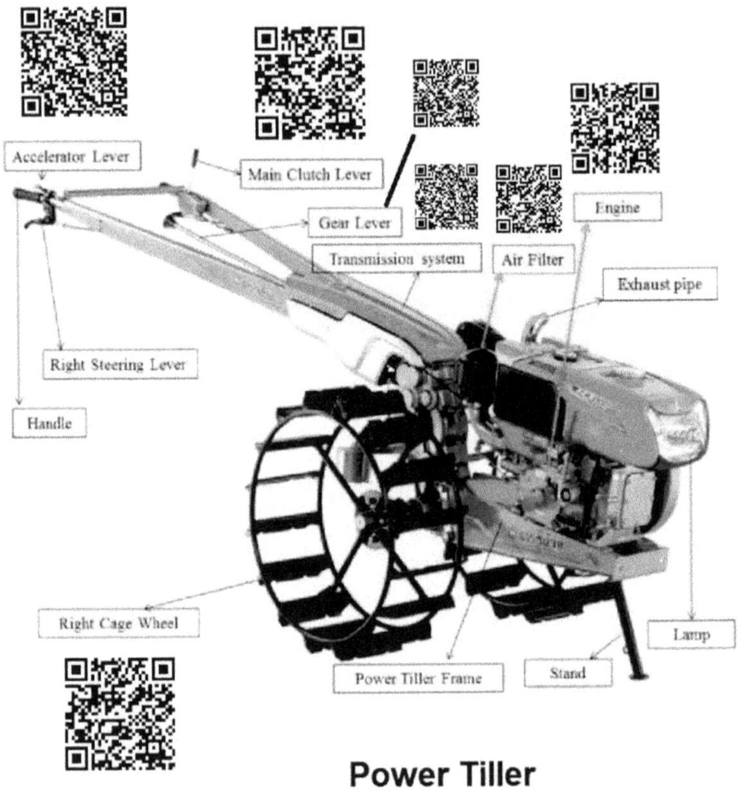

Power Tiller

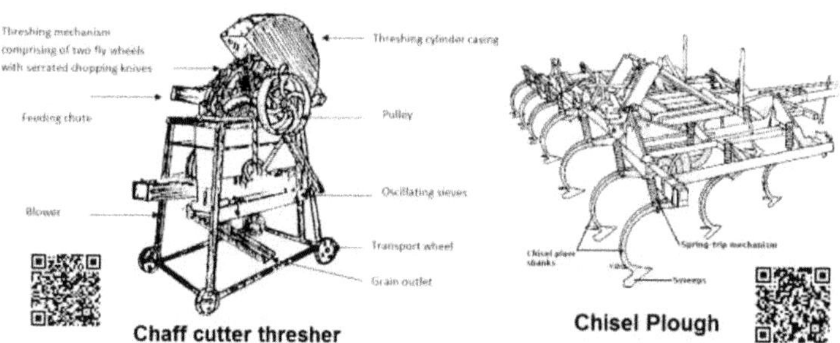

Chaff cutter thresher

Chisel Plough

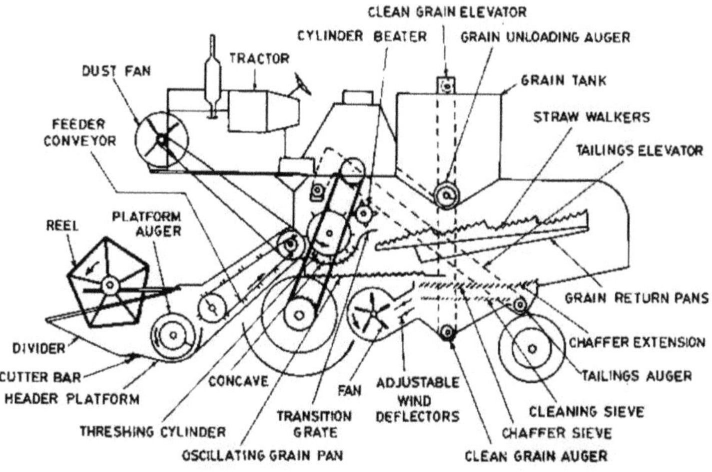

Combine harvester

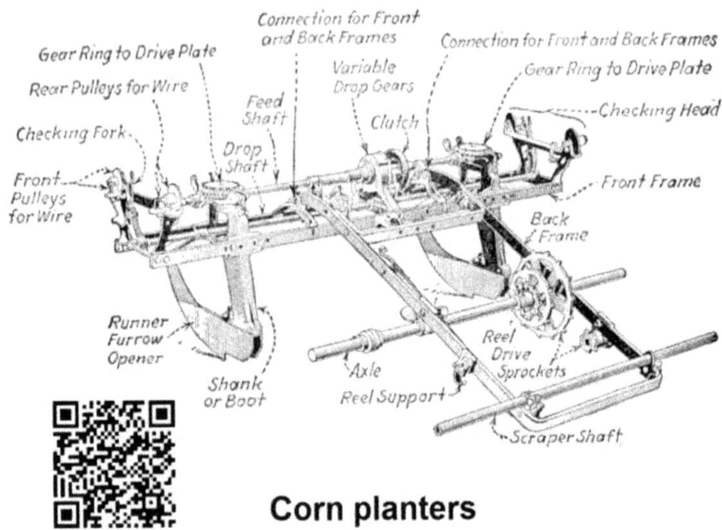

Corn planters

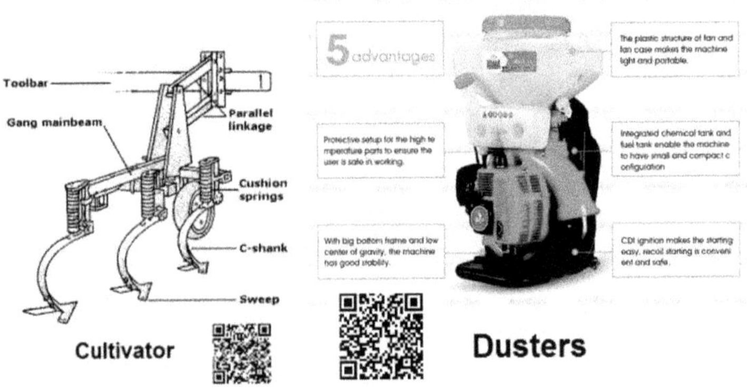

Cultivator

Dusters

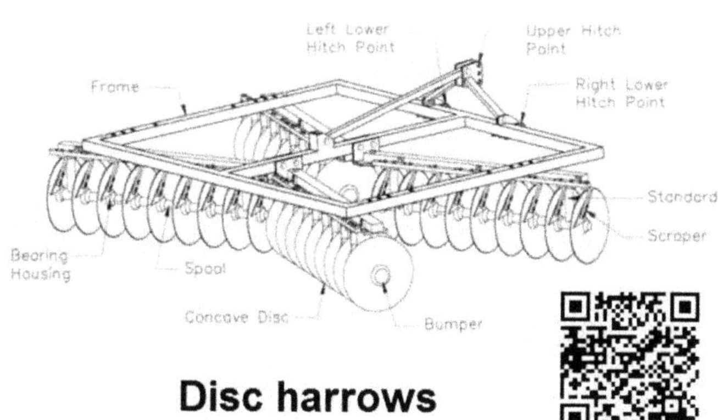
Left Lower
Hitch Point
Upper Hitch
Point
Frame
Right Lower
Hitch Point
Standard
Scraper
Bearing
Housing
Spool
Concave Disc
Bumper
Disc harrows

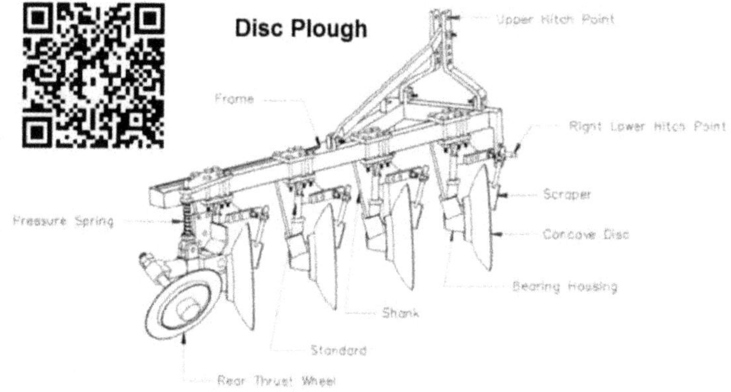
Disc Plough
Upper Hitch Point
Frame
Right Lower Hitch Point
Scraper
Pressure Spring
Concave Disc
Bearing Housing
Shank
Standard
Rear Thrust Wheel

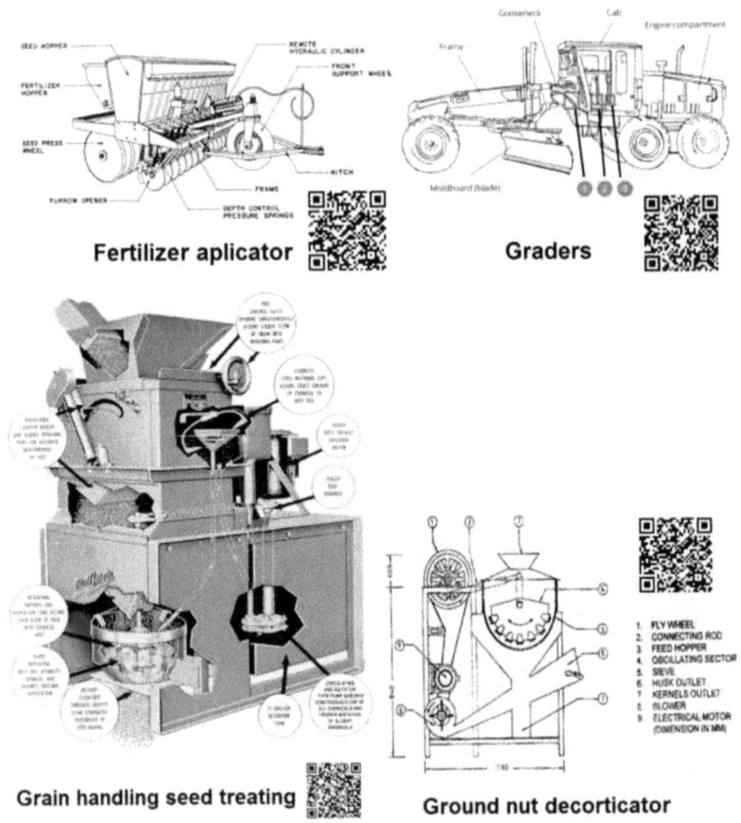

Fertilizer aplicator

Graders

Grain handling seed treating

Ground nut decorticator

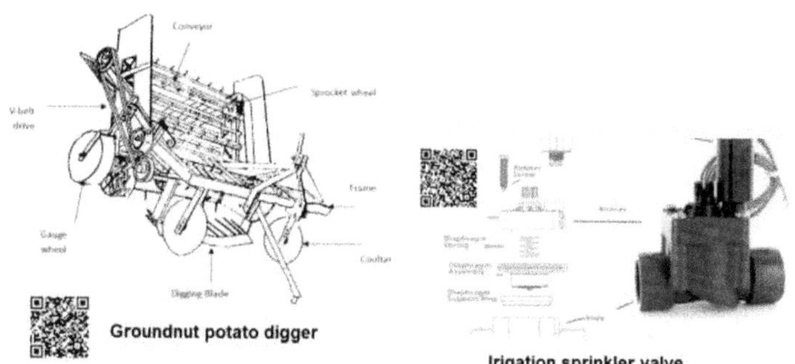

Groundnut potato digger

Irigation sprinkler valve

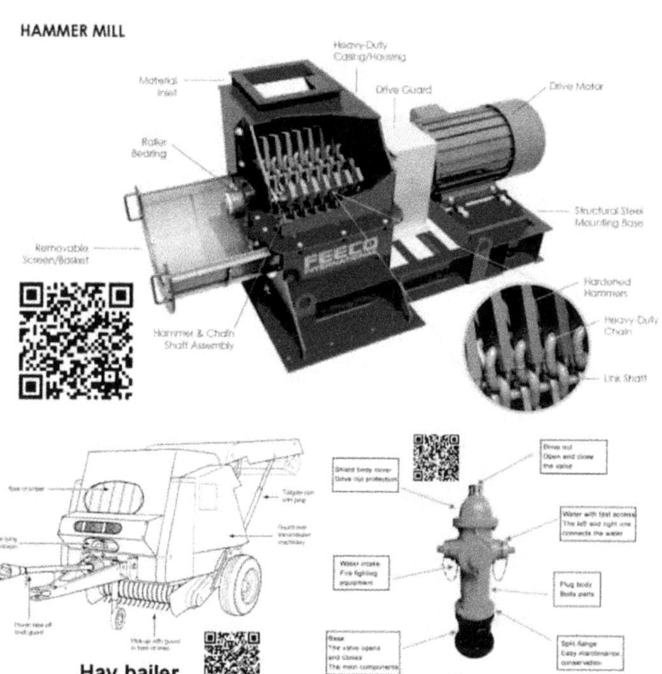

Hay bailer

Hydrants

Lazar leveler

Maize seller

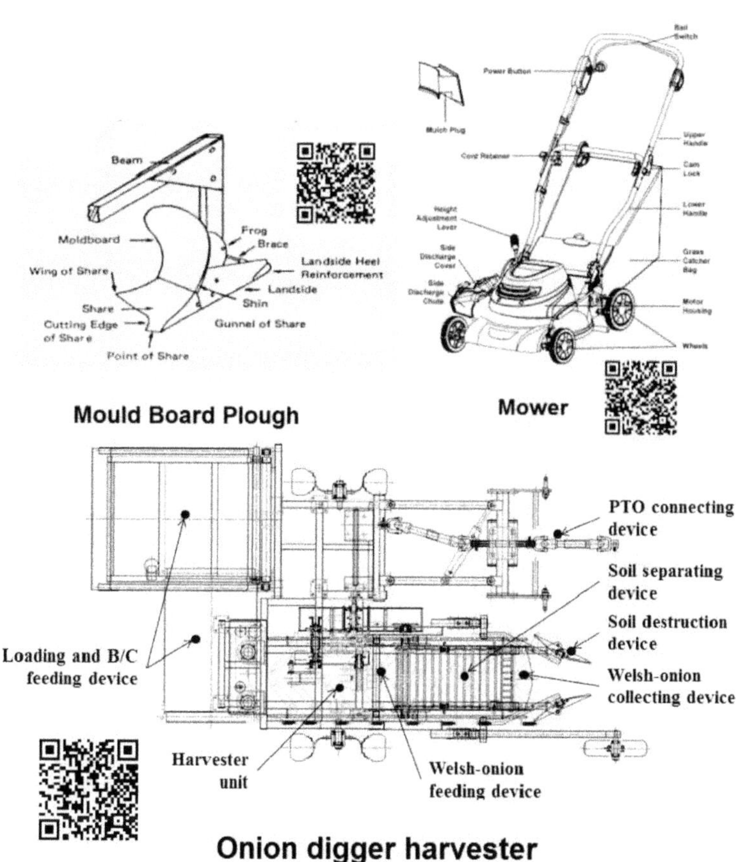

Mould Board Plough

Mower

Onion digger harvester

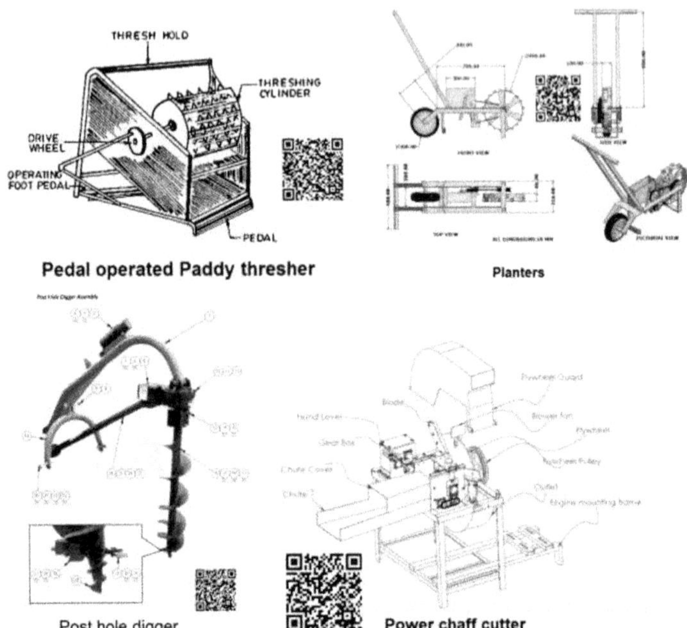

Pedal operated Paddy thresher

Planters

Post hole digger

Power chaff cutter

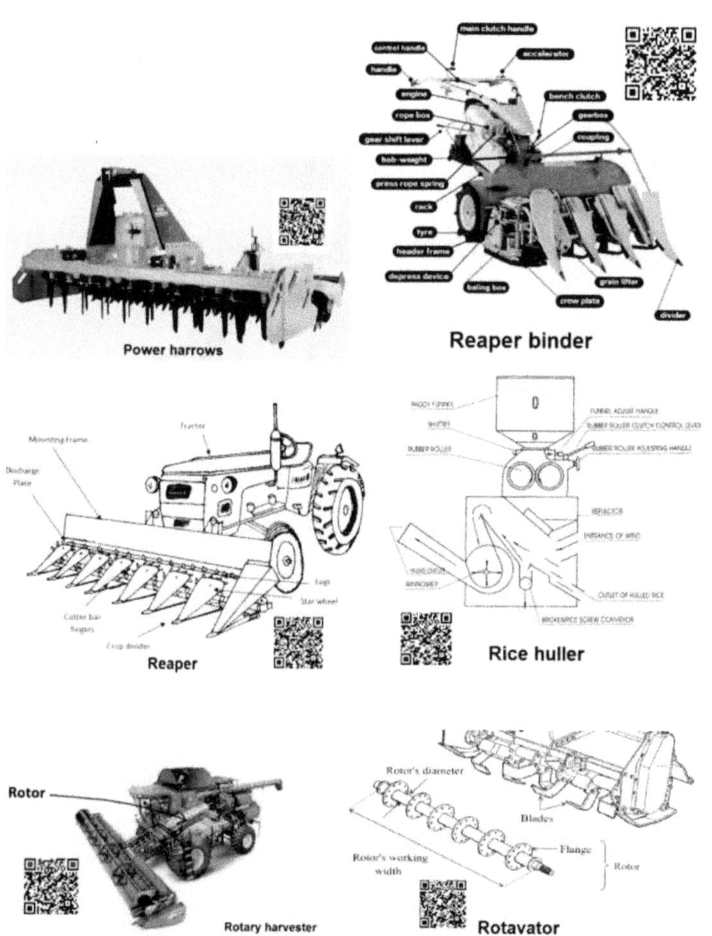
Power harrows
main clutch handle
control handle
accelerator
handle
engine
bench clutch
rope box
gearbox
gear shift lever
coupling
bob-weight
press rope spring
rack
tyre
header frame
depress device
baling box
grain lifter
crow plate
divider
Reaper binder
Tractor
Mounting Frame
Discharge Plate
Lugs
Star wheel
Crop divider
Reaper
Rice huller
Rotor
Rotary harvester
Rotor's diameter
Blades
Flange
Rotor's working width
Rotor
Rotavator

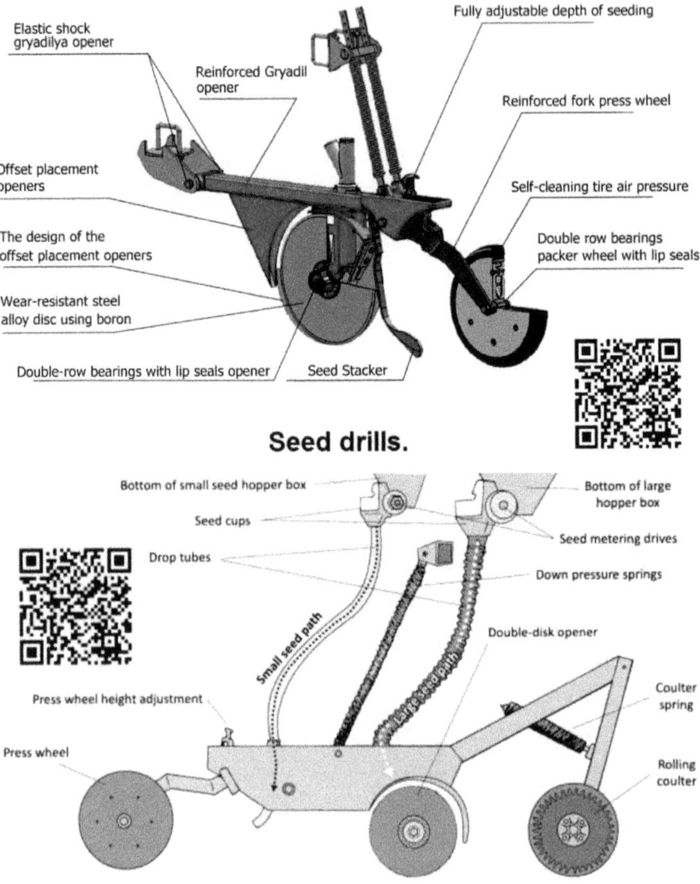

Seed drills.

Seed drills

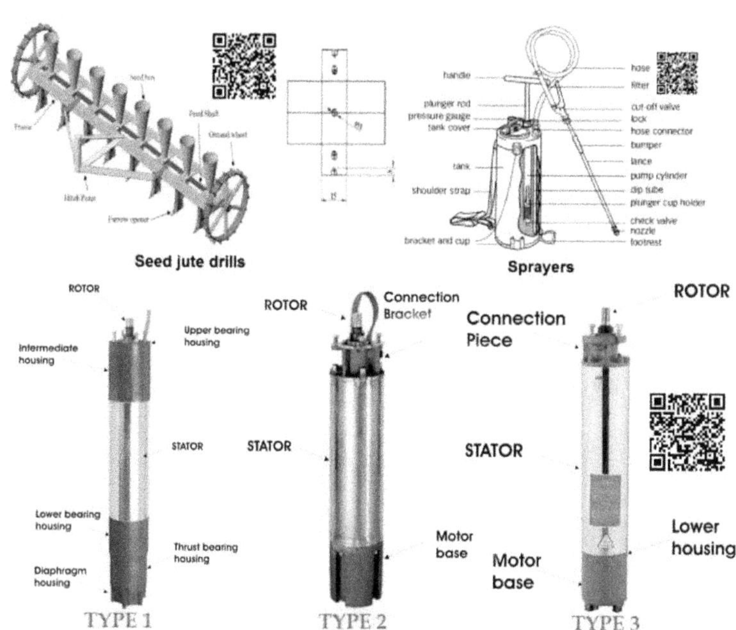

Seed jute drills

Sprayers

Submersible pump

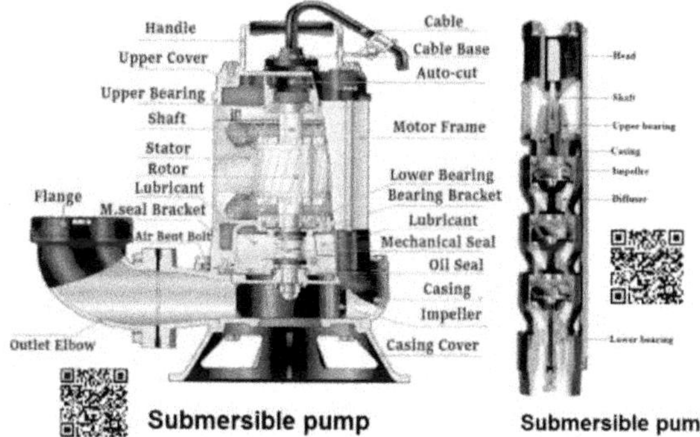

Submersible pump

Submersible pump

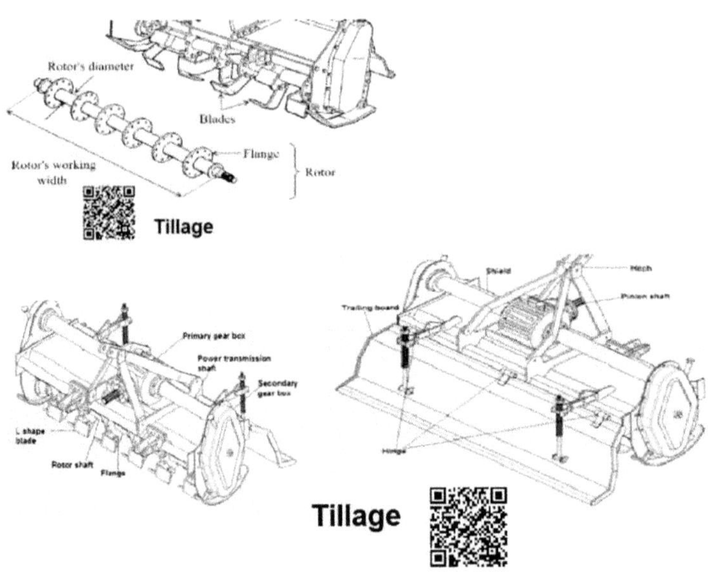
Rotor's diameter
Blades
Flange
Rotor
Rotor's working width
Tillage
Primary gear box
Power transmission shaft
Secondary gear box
L shape blade
Rotor shaft
Flange
Shield
Trailing board
Hinge
Tillage

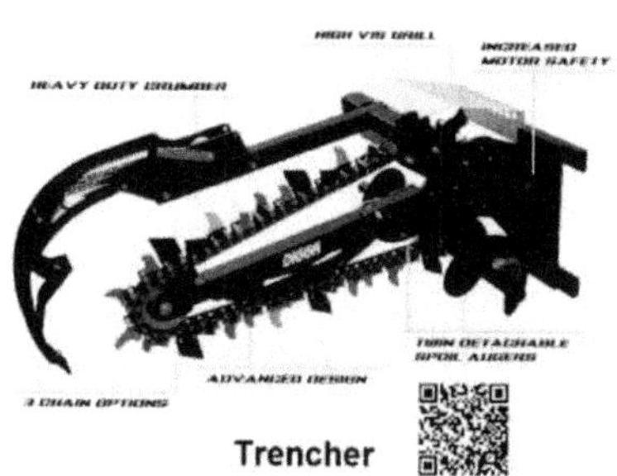
Trencher

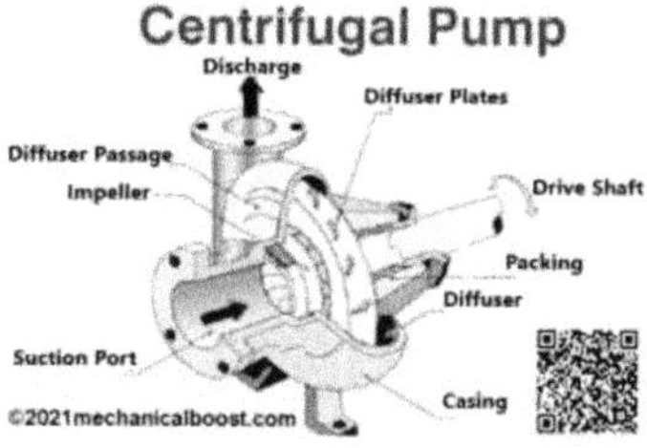

volute type centrifugal pump

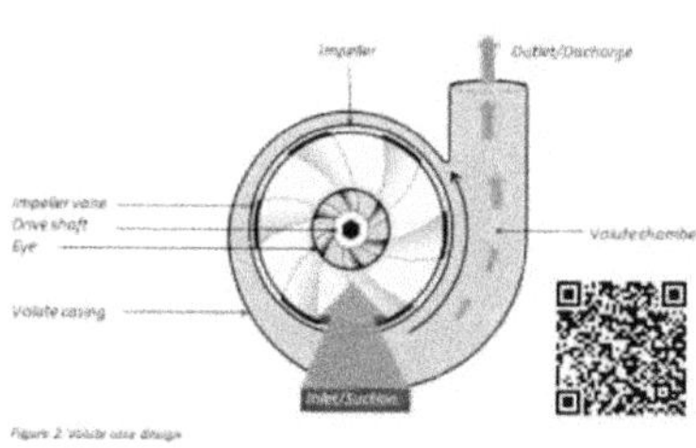
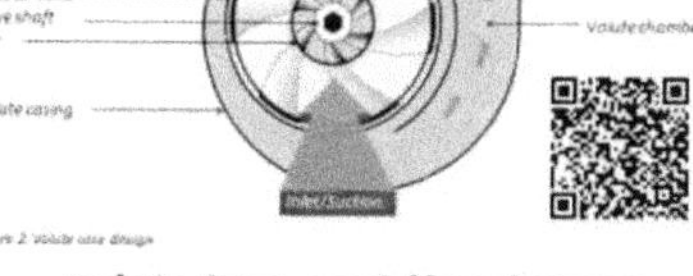

volute type centrifugal pump

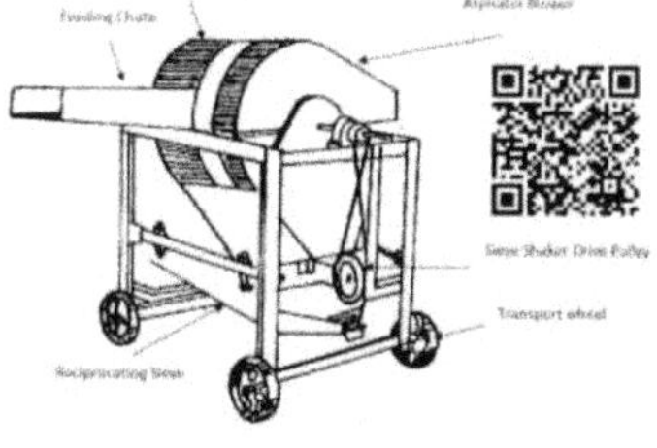
wheat Thresher

CHAPTER TWO

Mechanic Agricultural Machinery Second Year MCQ

1] Which classification of tillage involves initial major soil working operation?

a) Secondary tillage

b) Primary tillage

c) Tertiary tillage

d) Primary & Secondary tillage

2] Which primary tillage operation is performed to cut, break and invert the soil partially or completely?

a) Ploughing

b) Winnowing

c) Threshing

d) Harrowing

3] What type of mouldboard is short but broader with a relatively abrupt curvature?

a) Sod or breaker

b) Slat

c) Stubble

d) General purpose

4] A flat plate which bears against and transmits lateral thrust of the plough bottom to the furrow wall is known as ___________

a) Landside

b) Tail piece

c) Jointer

d) Coulter

5] Which plough accessory is used to turn over a small ribbon like furrow slice directly in front of the main plough bottom?

a) Coulter

b) Gauge wheel

c) Jointer

d) Land wheel

6] Reversible ploughs which have single bottom with such an arrangement that the plough bottom is changed from right hand to left hand by rotating it approximately 180°?

a) Turn Wrest plough

b) Disc plough

c) Chisel plough

d) Rotavator

7] What is the disc angle of a good plough?

a) 35°-39°

b) 42°-45°

c) 23°-27°

d) 59°-63°

8] Which plough is the combination of principles of the regular disc plough and the disc harrow and is used for shallow working in the soil?

a) Vertical disc plough

b) Chisel plough

c) Subsoiler

d) Standard disc plough

9] Which plough is used to cut and pulverise soil by impact forces by means of a number of rotary tynes or knives?

a) Rotating auger plough

b) Rotavator

c) Chisel plough

d) Rotary plough

10] A strip of land left unploughed at each end of the field for the tractor to turn is known as ________

a) Head land

b) Dead furrow

c) Back furrow

d) Crown

1] Which part of mould board plough invert the furrow slice to cover threshes?

A] Plough bottom

B] Land side

C] Mould board

D] Cross shaft

2] Which material used to make the part frog of plough?

A] Stain less steel

B] High carbon steel

C] High speed steel

D] Cast iron

3] What is the type of hitch point?

A] Two point hitch

B] Single point hitch

C] Three point hitch

D] Four point hitch

4] What is the type of hitch system?

A] Two point hitch system

B] Single point hitch system

C] Three point hitch system

D] Four point hitch system

5] Which method of ploughing the plough works round a strip of ploughed land?

A] Gathering

B] Casting

C] Tilling

D] Hitching

6] Which ploughing method practiced for fields showing higher elevation in centre?

A] Gathering

B] Hitching

C] Casting

D] Primary tillage

7] Which ploughing method saves fuel and time?

A] Gathering method

B] Mixed method

C] Casting method

D] Hitching method

8] What is the maintance activity to be carried out during storage of mould board plough?

A] Bar points to be checked with radious gauge

B] Clean the coulters with petrol jelly

C] Soil engage parts to be coated with anti-rust compound

D] Coulter edges tobe lubricated

9] Which tool is used to check the bar point / share of mould board plough?

A] Feeler gauge

B] Parallel blocks

C] Steel rule

D] Stright edge

10] What is the name of attaching the implements with the tractor for field operation?

A] Ploughing

B] Harvesting

C] Hitching

D] Seed planting

11] What is the objective of primary tillage operation?

A] Provide support to disc plough

B] Deep ploughing for reclamation work

C] Good seed bed preparation

D] Helps in breaking up hard pan

12] Which operation performed on the soil before and after seed placement?

A] Primary tillage

B] Secondary tillage

C] Ploughing head land

D] Gathering

13] Which type of operation destroy the weeds and prevent their growth?

A] Tillage operation

B] Hitching operation

C] Rotavator operation

D] Seed drilling operation

14] Which among the following implement used for tillage operation?

A] Sub soiler

B] Rotavator

C] Harrow ploughs

D] scraper

15] What is the type of agriculture implement?

A] Leveller

B] Mould board plough

C] Scraper

D] Ridger

1] What percentages of carbon are present in share of a mouldboard?

a) 0]70%-0]80%

b) 0]50%-0]60%

c) 0]30%-0]40%

d) 0]10%-0]20%

2] A bullock drawn desi plough is working at 2]4 KMPH and cutting soil 20 cm deep and 20 cm wide furrow at top] Calculate the volume of soil cut in 5h]

a) 248 m3

b) 219 m3

c) 240 m3

d) 200 m3

3] A pair of bullocks exert 100 kg pull at 30° to the horizontal while making a V-shape furrow 15 cm wide and 5 cm deep] The speed of ploughing is 3 KMPH] What is the unit draft on the implement and horsepower developed by the bullocks?

a) 2]31 kg/cm2; 0]96 HP

b) 2]11 kg/cm2; 0]86 HP

c) 2]56 kg/cm2; 0]98 HP

d) 3]11 kg/cm2; 0]76 HP

4] A two-wheel drive tractor pulls an implement which requires a draft of 12]5 KN] The motion resistance of the tractor is 4]5 KN and the slip of the driver wheel is 20%] The transmission efficiency is 0]8] the percentage of power lost in converting engine power into drawbar power is _______

a) 26]47%

b) 36%

c) 41]18%

d) 52]94%

5] What percentage of manganese are present in the share of a mouldboard?

a) 0]50%-0]80%

b) 0]90%-1%

c) 0]20%-0]40%

d) 0]10%-0]30%

6] Which share has a detachable piece?

a) Slip share
b) Slipnose share
c) Shin share
d) Bar point share

7] Which mouldboard has gentle curvature which lifts and inverts the unbroken furrow slice?

a) Slat type
b) General purpose type
c) Sod or breaker type
d) Stubble type

8] Gunnel is which face of the share that slides along the furrow wall?

a) Vertical
b) Horizontal
c) Centre
d) Parallel

9] Which share has the disadvantage of replacing the entire share if it gets worn out?

a) Bar point share
b) Shin share
c) Slipnose share
d) Slip share

10] Horizontal suction varies according to ______

a) Line of pull
b) Size of plough
c) Draft
d) Centre of power

16] What is the name of agriculture implement?

A] Sub soiler
B] Furrow wheel
C] Disc plough
D] Mould board plough

17] What is the function of sub soiler?

A] Harrvesting grain crops
B] Break the lower impermeable hard pan
C] Levelling the field
D] Stabilize the rear plough

18] What is the purpose of single standard sub soiler?

A] Used for shallower operation

B] Used for levelling operation

C] Used for deeper depth

D] Used for fertilizer application

19] Why the shank of sub soiler have several holes drilled in its sides?

A] To hold wings and sweeps

B] For lubrication

C] Reduce weight

D] Provide clearance

20] Which type of agriculture implement used for incorporating straw and green manure in the field?

A] Harrows

B] Rotavator

C] Cultivator

D] Sub soiler

21] What is the type of agriculture implement?

A] Cultivator

B] Harrows

C] Rotavator

D] Sub soiler

22] Which type of rotavator blade kill weeds and cause less pulverization?

A] L - shape blade

B] C- shape blade

C] Speed blade

D] Stright knife blade

23] Which blade is recommended for heavy wet soil in the rotavator?

A] C- shape blade

B] L - shape blade

C] Stright knife blade

D] Speed blade

24] What is the purpose of using longer shank blade in the rotavator?

A] For deeper cultivation

B] For levelling the field

C] For seed bed preparation

D] For shallow ploughing operation

25] Which agriculture implement used for preparing seed bed in a single pass both in dry and wet land conditions?

A] Scraper

B] Harvester

C] Ditcher

D] Rotavator

26] What is the purpose of cultivator?

A] Used for primary tillage operation

B] Used for secondary tillage operation

C] Tilling the soil between row corps

D] Used for Deep cultivation

27] What is the material used to make Tyne of cultivator?

A] High carbon steel

B] Mild steel

C] Low carbon steel

D] Stainless steel

28] What is the purpose of two heavy coil springs provided in the Tyne of cultivator

A] Provide cushioning effect

B] Prevent damage in case of obstacle

C] Adjust the Tyne angle

D] Provide smooth operation

29] What is the name of agriculture machinery?

A] Disc plough

B] Mould board plough

C] Cultivator

D] Disc harrow

30] Which type of agriculture implement used to prevent surface evaporation loss?

A] Disc plough

B] Rotavator

C] Cultivator

D] Disc harrow

1] Which plough is used is used to break Hard pan or plough sole layer of soil?

a) Subsoiler

b) Chisel plough

c) Rotavator

d) Rotating auger plough

2] How is effect of speed on draft expressed?

a) Ds = D0 + KS2

b) Ds = D0 – KS2

c) Ds = D0 * KS2

d) Ds = D0 / KS2

3] In order to provide furrows at all times on the right-hand side of the plough which method/methods is/are used?

a) Gathering

b) Casting

c) Gathering and casting

d) None of the above

4] What is the depreciated value after n years using declining balance method?

a) D = P(1-r)n

b) D = P(1/r)n

c) D = P(1*r)n

d) D = P(1+r)n

5] What is the Break Even Point?

a) Uc = Fcx*Ox

b) Uc = Fcx+Ox

c) Uc = Fcx-Ox

d) Uc = Fc*x*Ox

6] What is the formula for computing depreciation in straight line method?

a) D = P-SL*H

b) D = P+SL*H

c) D = P-SL+H

d) D = (P-S)*(L*H)

7] What are the ways of doing round and round ploughing?

a) Starting at the outer end

b) Starting at the centre

c) Back furrowing

d) Starting at the outer end & starting at the centre

8] What is distance of centre of resistance from share wing?

a) $3/4^{th}$ size of plough

b) $3/4^{th}$ size of share

c) $3/4^{th}$ size of tractor

d) $3/4^{th}$ size of frog

1] The flanged tube, mounted on the gang axle between every two discs to retain them at fixed position laterally on the shaft is called _______

a) Spool
b) Gang
c) Bearing
d) Scraper

2] Which disc harrow has two gangs in tandem and two fitted one behind the other?

a) Tractor drawn
b) Off set
c) Tandem
d) Double action

31] What is the use of harrows?

A] For seed bed preparation before planting
B] Used after seed bed preparation
C] Used for penetrating hard ground
D] Used for Deep cultivation

32] What is the cause for excessive noise from tiller?

A] Rotor speed too high
B] Gear box oil level too low
C] Blade bolt not tight
D] Soil too wet to work

33] How to remove end play from wheels of cultivator?

A] Provide take up washer
B] Provide balancing weights
C] Adjust with bolt and nut
D] Adjust the shovels to uniform depth

34] How the shovels are secured with tynes?

A] By bolt and nut
B] By riveting
C] By welding
D] By clamps

35] What is the thickness of disc blades of harrows in general?

A] 5 mm to 11 mm
B] 3 mm to 9 mm
C] 7 mm to 12 mm
D] 6 mm to 12 mm

36] What is the material used to make 'Spool' in disc harrows?

A] Stainless steel
B] High carbon steel

C] Cast iron

D] Wrought iron

37] What is the name of arrangement of gangs placed one behind the other?

A] Single action

B] Double action

C] Offset arrangement

D] Multi action

38] Which factor affects the disc harrows penetration?

A] Thickness of harrow

B] Arrangement of harrow

C] Material of harrow

D] Weight of harrow

39] What is the type of harrow?

A] Spike tooth harrow

B] Spring tooth harrow

C] Drag harrow

D] Blade harrow

40] What is the name of harrow?

A] Drag harrow

B] Disc harrow

C] Blade harrow

D] ACME harrow

41] What is the shape of disc harrow blades?

A] Convex

B] Square

C] Concave

D] Radious

3] What is the size of the discs in tractor drawn disc harrows?

a) 20-30 cm diameter

b) 10-30 cm diameter

c) 90-110 cm diameter

d) 35-70 cm diameter

4] What is the weight of the disc harrow?

a) 80 to 100 kg

b) 30 to 50 kg

c) 10 to 40 kg

d) 23 to 56 kg

5] What is the range of the gang angle?

a) 29°-39°

b) 34°-56°

c) <u>0°-27°</u>

d) 89°-100°

6] Which harrow is known as knife harrow?

a) Patela

b) Spring tooth harrow

c) Triangular harrow

d) <u>Acme harrow</u>

7] How many acres can be covered by a harrow of 1]5 m width in a day of 8 hours with bullock power] If each spike of the harrow is giving 1 kg resistance when there are 50 spikes] What power would be necessary for the bullocks to pull the harrow?

a) <u>0]544 KW</u>

b) 0]987 KW

c) 0]123 KW

d) 0]333 KW

8] What power is necessary for pulling a harrow with 50 times, each giving a resistance of 1 kg, when the speed of harrow is 5km/hr]

a) 0]980 KW

b) 0]223 KW

c) <u>0]680 KW</u>

d) 1]902 KW

1] Which of the following is not a type of a cultivator?

a) Disc

b) Rotary

c) Tine

d) <u>Off-set</u>

2] A five-tine cultivator having tine spacing 8cm, working depth of 5cm and speed is 3km/hr] Turning loss is 10%] Soil resistance is 0]6 kg/cm2] Width of furrow is 5 cm] What will be the maximum draft?

a) 106 kg

b) <u>120 kg</u>

c) 186 kg

d) 116 kg

3] A tractor is attached with a 9-tine cultivator] While field testing, drawbar dynamometer shows an average pull of 14000 N] the speed of tractor is 6 km per hour] Find the power of the tractor]

a) 24 KW
b) 25 KW
c) 21]67 KW
d) 23]33 KW

4] What is the cutting angle range of a shovel?

a) 15°-20°
b) 34°-39°
c) 45°-49°
d) 50°-60°

5] What is the angle made by the three openings at the bottom of the funnel?

a) 110°
b) 100°
c) 106°
d) 120°

6] What are the dimensions of a duck foot cultivator?

a) 225 cm long; 60 cm wide; 7 sweeps
b) 106 cm long; 90 cm wide; 7 sweeps
c) 120 cm long; 60 cm wide; 6 sweeps
d) 215 cm long; 50 cm wide; 10 sweeps

7] Which cultivators are operated by the tractors which are fitted with hydraulic lift?

a) Trailed cultivator
b) Mounted cultivator
c) Cultivator with spring loaded tines
d) Cultivator with rigid tines

8] In which cultivator, the spacing of the tines are changed by slackening and sliding of bolts?

a) Cultivator with rigid tines
b) Cultivator with spring loaded tines
c) Duck foot cultivator
d) Mounted cultivator

9] A three-tine cultivator having tine spacing 6 cm, working depth of 3 cm and speed is 2 km/hr] Turning loss is 10%] Soil resistance is 0]6 kg/cm2] Width of furrow is 6 cm] What will be the required power?

a) 0]54 KW
b) 0]23 KW

c) 0]17 KW

d) 1 KW

42] What will be the effect of increasing disc gang angle of disc harrow?

A] Decrease penetration

B] Improve penetration

C] Ensure effective levelling

D] Breaking hard soil of land

43] Which type of harrow is used in hard and stony soil?

A] Spike tooth harrow

B] Spring tooth harrow

C] Drag harrow

D] Disc harrow

44] What is the advantage of disc plough compared with mould board plough?

A] Facilitate deep aultivation

B] Cover the area with faster speed

C] Speed can be varied

D] Break the hard soil effectively

45] What is the name of disc plough accessory?

A] Beam

B] Hitching unit

C] Disc assembly

D] Rear furrow wheel

46] Which angles of disc plough are responsible for desired penetration in the soil?

A] Cross shaft and crank angle

B] Disc and tilt angle

C] Beam frame angle

D] Furrow wheel and ground wheel angle

47] What is the recommended disc and tilt angle of disc plough?

A] 46° and 22°

B] 42° and 18°

C] 38° and 12°

D] 24° and 12°

48] What is the type of agriculture implement?

A] Bund maker

B] Bed farmer

C] Leveller

D] Ditcher
49] What is the name of agriculture implement?
A] Ditcher
B] Terracer
C] Bund maker
D] Scraper
50] What is the name of agriculture implement?
A] Digger
B] Cultivator
C] Terracer
D] Dumper
51] What is the name of agriculture implement?
A] Digger
B] Dumper
C] Terracer
D] Scraper
52] Which power system drives post hole digger?
A] Hydraulic system
B] Pneumatic system
C] Mechanical system
D] Electrical system
53] What is the use of post hole digger?
A] Dig multiple holes for fence posts
B] Deep cultivation
C] Tilling the soil between row corps
D] Grading and levelling of fields
54] What is the name of agriculture implement?
A] Scraper
B] Pest hole digger
C] Cultivator
D] Dumper
55] Which agriculture equipment used for rough levelling and cutting of high spots?
A] Scraper
B] Dumper
C] Leveller
D] Digger
56] What is the use of scraper?

A] Loading and unloading soil from one place to other

B] Deep cultivation

C] Tilling the soil between row corps

D] Prepare the land by breaking clods

57] What is the type of agriculture implement?

A] Scraper

B] Dumper

C] Leveller

D] Cultivator

1] In which process of seeding, the seeds are placed in the holes made in seed bed and covering them?

a) Broadcasting

b) Transplanting

c) Dibbling

d) Drilling

2] Which of the following is not a type of Drilling?

a) Sowing behind the plough

b) Bullock drawn seed drills

c) Tractor drawn seed drills

d) Check row planting

3] In which seed metering mechanism, the feed wheel is provided with fine and coarse ribbed flanges?

a) Internal double run type

b) Fluted feed type

c) Cell feed mechanism

d) Brush feed mechanism

4] Calculate the cost of seeding one hectare of land with bullock-drawn seed drill of 5*22 cm size] The speed of bullocks is 3km/hr] Hire charges of bullocks ? 100/- per pair, hire charges of seed drill is ? 50/- per day and wage of operator ? 100/- per day of 8 hours]

a) ? 84]88

b) ? 94]68

c) ? 110]90

d) ? 34]29

5] A fluted feed seed drill has eight furrow openers of single disc type] The furrow openers are spaced 25 cm apart and the main drive wheel has a diameter of 120 cm] How many turns of main drive wheel would occur when the seed drill has covered one hectare of area?

a) 1333]3
b) 1666]6
c) 1999]9
d) 1234]5

6] Calculate the time required for sowing 1]6 hectares of land by five furrows seed drill going 12]5 cm deep] The speed of seed drill is 3]2 km/hr and pressure exerted by the soil on the seed drill is 0]42 kg/cm2] The space between furrow openers is 10 cm and loss in turning is 10%]

a) 21]07 hrs
b) 9]87 hrs
c) 2]34 hrs
d) 11]11 hrs

7] Calculate the seed rate/hectare of a 7*17 cm seed drill, whose main drive wheel is 124 cm diameter and total weight of grain collected in 20 revolutions in 0]423 kg]

a) 45]58 kg
b) 54]34 kg
c) 90 kg
d) 23]78 kg

8] Maximum yield of maize is obtained with a population of 40000 plants per hectare] The rows are 140cm apart and an average emergence of 85% is expected] How many seeds per hill should be planted if hills are 140cm apart?

a) 9
b) 2
c) 10
d) 11

9] Which seed metering mechanism consists of cups of spoon on the periphery of a vertical rotating disc?

a) Cup feed mechanism
b) Cell feed mechanism
c) Brush feed mechanism
d) Picker wheel mechanism

10] Which seeding method uses Malobansa?

a) Transplanting
b) Seed dropping behind the plough
c) Check row planting
d) Hill dropping

1] Which of the following is not a type of furrow opener?

a) Shovel type

b) Shoe type

c) Disc type

d) <u>Brush feed type</u>

58] What is the material used to make the blade of leveller?

A] High carbon steel

B] <u>Medium carbon steel</u>

C] Low carbon steel

D] Stain less steel

59] Which agriculture equipment used for uniform distribution of water in the field?

A] Scraper

B] Dumper

C] <u>Leveller</u>

D] Tiller

60] What is the name of soil forming equipment?

A] Dumper

B] <u>Leveller</u>

C] Scraper

D] Hole digger

61] What is the use of trenchers?

A] <u>Laying pipes and making tunnels</u>

B] Deep cultivation

C] Loading and unloading of soil

D] Clean the mud from auger

62] What is the periodical oil change in the gear box unit and transmission unit of ditcher?

A] <u>30 Hrs</u>

B] 50 Hrs

C] 60 Hrs

D] 80 Hrs

63] What is the type of furrow opener?

A] Single disc opener

B] <u>Double Disc type</u>

C] Hoe type

D] Shoe type

64] What is the purpose of furrow opener?

A] Used to store the seed in machine

B] Open a furrow in the soil at uniform depth

C] Used for deep cultivation

D] Uniform spreading of seeds

65] Which part of fertilizer applicator ensures High degree of uniforming in sowing?

A] Spiral tubes

B] Rubber tubes

C] Polythene tubes

D] Telescopic tubes

66] What is the advantage of using polythene or rubber tubes in the fertilizer applicator?

A] Clogging and choking easily detectable

B] Flexibility in usage

C] Easy Handling

D] Reduction of weight

67] what is the advantage of serrated disc in the fertilizer applicator?

A] Prevent the gravitational flow fertilizer

B] Maintain the constant speed

C] Crushing the small clods of fertilizer

D] Provide uniform spreading of fertilizer

68] What is the name of device in fetilizer applicator?

A] Spur wheel

B] Ground wheel

C] Star wheel

D] Serrated disc

69] Why the spur wheel of fertilizer applicator width is more than the notch?

A] Prevent gravitation flow of fertilizer at rest

B] Provide uniform flow of fertilizer

C] prevent stucking of spur wheel

D] Increase the speed of spur wheel

70] What is the material used to make spur wheel of fetilizer metering device?

A] Castiron

B] High carbon steel

C] Aluminium casting

D] stainless steel

2] Which of the following is not a type of a Shovel?

a) Reversible

b) Spear point

c) Reciprocating power

d) Single point

3] What is the minimum carbon content and thickness of Shoe type furrow?

a) 0]5% and 4mm

b) 0]5% and 2mm

c) 0]2% and 4mm

d) 0]8% and 8mm

4] What is the minimum diameter of seed and fertilizer tube in disc type furrow opener?

a) 30mm

b) 45mm

c) 60mm

d) 25mm

5] Which furrow opener has toe and 'T' shaped scrapers?

a) Reversible shovel

b) Double disc type

c) Spear point shovel

d) Single disc type

6] What is the range of the implement used in cultivator with seeding attachment?

a) 600-700mm

b) 400-500mm

c) 100-200mm

d) 900-1000mm

7] Which seed metering device mechanism in a planter brushes out excess seeds from the cells of the feed mechanism?

a) Edge drop

b) Cut off

c) Knock out

d) Flat drop

8] What is the field capacity of a potato planter (semi-automatic)?

a) 0]15-0]25 ha/hr

b) 0]10-0]14 ha/hr

c) 0]40-0]55 ha/hr

d) 0]09-0]14 ha/hr

9] Which planter has six C-type blades on its flanges?

a) Potato planter

b) Low land paddy seeder

c) Rice trans planter

d) Zero till drill

10] What is the capacity of potato planter (Automatic)?

a) 1000-4000 potatoes/hour

b) 200-900 potatoes/hour

c) 6000-14000 potatoes/hour

d) 16000-32000 potatoes/hour

1] At what height should the transplanting be done in paddy?

a) 5-10 cm

b) 15-20 cm

c) 45-50 cm

d) 30-35 cm

2] What should be the spacing of paddy in the sub-normal conditions?

a) 15*10 cm2

b) 24*12 cm2

c) 34*24 cm2

d) 8*12 cm2

71] What is the name of agriculture implement?

A] Fertilizer Applicator

B] Marking roller

C] Automatic planter

D] Sugarcane planter

72] Which is the essential factor of fertilizer applicator?

A] Application rate should be adjustable

B] Application speed should be constant

C] Fertilizer applicator should be simple in construction

D] Easy replacement of defective parts

73] Why furrow opener becomes heavy and accumulated with seed and soil in the planter?

A] Fertilizer not properly metered

B] Improper sowing rate

C] Improper seed bed preparation

D] Dis placement of seed

74] What will be the effect in reverse operation of vegetable transplanter?

A] Furrow opener will be bend

B] Furrow opener will be filled with soil

C] Furrow opener will break

D] Displacement of seed in the furrow

75] What is the formula used to calculate sowing rate?

A] Kg seed per ha=(D x W)/P

B] Kg seed per ha=(D +W)/P

C] Kg seed per ha=(D - W)/P

D] Kg seed per ha=(W - D)/P

76] Which planting allows the soil to dry rapidly and gaurds againts excess moisture?

A] Flat planting

B] Bed planting

C] Furrows planting

D] Blisters planting

77] Which crop is suitable for ridge planting?

A] Maize

B] Cotton

C] sugarcane

D] Potato

78] Which method of planting followed for maize crops?

A] Flat land planting

B] Ridge planting

C] Furrow planting

D] Vertical land planting

79] What is the speed of sugarcane planter?

A] 0]4 - 4 km/hr

B] 0]8 - 5 km/hr

C] 0]6 - 7 km/hr

D] 0]5 - 5 km/hr

80] What is the row spacing of rice crops?

A] 20 x 10 cm

B] 25 x 15 cm

C] 20 x 20 cm

D] 25 x 20 cm

81] What is the name of planter?

A] Corn planter

B] Potato planter

C] Paddy planter

D] <u>Vegetable trans planter</u>

82] What is the purpose of inclined press wheels in the vegetable trans planter?

A] Spacing the trans plantation

B] <u>Firm soil around the root</u>

C] Maintain the depth of plant

D] Changing the planting depth

83] What is the spacing distance between the rows to be maintained in power tiller mounted rice planting?

A] 10 cm

B] 15 cm

C] <u>20 cm</u>

D] 25 cm

84] How the tray movement mechanism achived in the manual paddy trans planting?

A] By worm gear and shaft

B] <u>By chain and free wheel</u>

C] By wheel and shaft

D] By rack and pinion

85] What is the name of planter?

A] Sugarcane planter

B] <u>cotton planter</u>

C] Potato planter

D] Two row multi crop planter

3] Which geometry has smothering effect on weeds?

a) Planting

b) Triangular

c) Circular

d) <u>Square</u>

4] How many seedlings per hill is recommended to transplant?

a) <u>6-7</u>

b) 7-8

c) <u>2-3</u>

d) 5-6

5] What should be the transplanting depth of paddy?

a) 2-3 cm
b) 4-5 cm
c) 8-9 cm
d) 6-7 cm

6] In which country the rice trans planters were developed?
a) India
b) Pakistan
c) China
d) Japan

7] Which part of the rice trans planter acts like a shed roof to the seedlings?
a) Seedling tray
b) Motor
c) Running gear
d) Gear box

8] The accuracy of the planter does not depend on _________
a) Speed of seed plate
b) Shape of hopper bottom
c) Uniformity of seed size
d) Weather

1] Which part operates the tractor drawn semi-mounted or mounted type mowers?
a) PTO shaft
b) Cutter
c) Pitman
d) Grass board

2] Which clutch is used in the driving unit of a mower?
a) Fluid coupling
b) Dog clutch
c) Friction clutch
d) Single plate

3] What is the difference between each knife clips?
a) 5-15 cm
b) 40-50 cm
c) 35-45 cm
d) 20-30 cm

4] When the knife section stops in the centre of its guard on every stroke, it is known as?

a) Re-embankment

b) Reinforcement

c) Registration

d) Rescue

5] Calculate the total time required to harvest 2]5 hectares of grass by means of a 2 metre mower being operated at 4 km/hr] (Field efficiency=80%)

a) 2]5 hrs

b) 1]2 hrs

c) 3]9 hrs

d) 7 hrs

6] What power is required to pull 1]2 mete mower working at a speed of 4]8 km/hr, if there is a load of 50 kg per metre length of mower and mechanical efficiency is 80%?

a) 1 KW

b) 0]98 KW

c) 0]23 KW

d) 2 KW

7] How many hectares per day of 10 hours can be cut by a combine with 4 metre cutter bar, when it is running at 4 k/hr?

a) 16ha

b) 20 ha

c) 28 ha

d) 8 ha

8] A mower has drive wheel of 60 cm diameter] The crank of the mower makes 600 rev/min when it is driven by a tractor, moving at a speed of 2]3 km/hr] If the speed ratio between the crank wheel and land wheel is changed to 27:1, calculate the increase in speed of mower to maintain same speed of crank]

a) 0]19 km/hr

b) 0]67 km/hr

c) 0]11 km/hr

d) 0]21 km/hr

9] Which part of mower is used to regulate the height of cut above the ground?

a) Ledger plate

b) Wearing plate

c) Shoe

d) Grass board

86] What is the type of planter?

A] Potato planter

B] Semi automatic planter

C] sugarcane planter

D] Cotton planter

87] How the spacing of seed is achieved in the semi automatic planter?

A] By changing the running wheel

B] By changing the feed ring

C] By adjusting furrow opener

D] By changing the direction of conveyer belt

88] What is the name of planter?

A] Two row multi crop planter

B] Three row multi crop planter

C] Automatic planter

D] Cotton planter

89] How many picker arms are attached with picker wheel of potato planter?

A] 12 Nos

B] 10 Nos

C] 8 Nos

D] 6 Nos

90] What is the type of planter?

A] Potato planter

B] Three row multi crop planter

C] Sugarcane planter

D] Two row multicrop planter

91] What is the cause of excessive vibration in the machine of happy seeder?

A] Broken flail blades

B] PTO shaft not engaging

C] Seed / fertilizer box empty

D] Fertilizer fluted roller is blocked

92] How much chloropyrophos to be added with seed to protect against termite attack in the happy seeder?

A] 2 ml / kg of seed

B] 3 ml / kg of seed

C] 4 ml / kg of seed

D] 5 ml / kg of seed

93] Which part of happy seeder regulate insertion of the furrow openers in to the soil to place seed at desired depth?

A] Drive wheel

B] Two depth control wheels

C] P]T]O shaft

D] Flail shaft

94] Where the fertilizwer box is mounted in the happy seeder?

A] Front side of frame

B] rear side of frame

C] Near the flail shaft

D] Top of frame

95] What is the purpose flail blades of furrow opener in the happy seeder?

A] Clean the furrow opener

B] Sharpen the tynes

C] Deliver the seed uniformly

D] Deliver the fertilizer evenly

96] What is the function of furrow opener in happy seeder?

A] Drill and place seed and fertilizer

B] Spread combine harvested rice straw

C] Control fertilizer application

D] Store the seed in the machine

97] Which agricultural implement combines stubble mulching and seed drilling in to one machine?

A] Cultivator

B] Happy seeder

C] Hand seed drill

D] Rotavator

98] Which type of seed & fertilizer device is used in drills for crops where seeds are easily damaged due to rough mechanical handling?

A] Cup type

B] Hoe type

C] Stub runner type

D] Full runner type

99] What is the provision is made for different sizes of seeds in the metering device?

A] Adjustable spring loaded baffle plate

B] Fluted rollar

C] Longitudinal grooves

D] Square shaft

1] Calculate the total time required to harvest 4 hectares of grass by means of a 2mm mower being operated at the speed of 4 km/h] Assume field efficiency of mower as 75%?

a) 4]67 hr

b) 5]67 hr

c) <u>6]67 hr</u>

d) 7]67 hr

2] What horsepower will be required to pull 1]2 m mower working at the speed of 5 km/m length of the mower ad mechanical efficiency is 85%?

a) <u>1]56</u>

b) 2]56

c) 3]56

d) 4]56

3] How many hectares of grass per day of 15 hours can be cut by a mower being operated at the speed of 4]5 km/h and with 4 m cutter bar]

a) 20

b) 22

c) <u>27</u>

d) 16

4] A mower has driven wheel of 60 cm diameter] The crank of mower makes 550 rpm, when it is driven by a tractor at a speed of 2 km/h] If speed ratio between the crank wheel and land wheel is changed to 27:1, calculate the increase in speed of mower to maintain the same speed of crank]

a) 0]20 km/h

b) <u>0]304 km/h</u>

c) 1]402 km/h

d) 1]36 km/h

5] A 2m mower is operating at 3]5 km/h with an overall efficiency of 75%] Calculate the area covered by it in ha/h]

a) <u>0]525</u>

b) 0]625

c) 0]725

d) 0]825

6] How many revolutions will each spindle of cotton picker make in the picking zone for a chain belt arrangement in which the speed of spindle is

1400 rpm and remains in the picking zone during 100 cm of forward travel]

a) 50

b) 21

c) 45

d) 11

7] A disc type mower is operated by PTO with 6 discs with a shaft of 0]4 m/disc] The specific energy required for cutting is 2]1 KJ/m2 and specific power losses due to air come stubble and gear train friction is 2 kw/m of cutting width] If the mower with tractor requires a propelling force of 2 KN the total power requirement for carrying out moving in Kw at forward speed of 3 km/h is ____

a) 10]67

b) 20]67

c) 30]67

d) 40]67

8] The most common mower, amongst the following is ____________

a) Reciprocating mower

b) Lawn mower

c) Cylindrical mower

d) Horizontal mower

9] A gang mower is the group of ____________

a) 2 or more cylindrical mowers

b) 5 mowers

c) 2 mowers

d) 10 mowers

10] In flail mower, the cutting section contains ____________

a) Cutter bar

b) Swinging knives

c) Fixed knives

d) Reciprocating fingers only

11] In cutter bar of mower, the knife head is attached to the ____________

a) Knife back

b) Cutter end

c) Starting point of cutting edge

d) Reciprocating fingers

12] In mower, the grass board is provided at the ____________

a) Cutter end

b) Knife end

c) Knife back

d) Reciprocating fingers

13] In cutter bar of mower, the knife sections are revitted to the ___________

a) Knife back

b) Reciprocating fingers

c) Stationary bar

d) Cylindrical drum

14] In mower, the pitman transmits the motion to the ___________

a) Knife head

b) Knife middle

c) Knife back

d) Knife end

15] Who invented the first lawn mower?

a) Albert Einstein

b) Buzz Aldrin

c) Edwin Budding

d) Yuri Gagarin

100] What is the type of seed & fertilizer metering device?

A] Fluted feed type

B] Cup type

C] Interuce double rum type

D] Sub rummer type

101] What is the type of seed drill?

A] Rubber belt precision seeder

B] Hand seed drill

C] Zero till drill seed cum fertilizer drill

D] Pneumatic seed drill

102] How the amount of seed sown is changed in seed cum fertilizer drill?

A] By shifting the roller sideways

B] By shifting the roller upper side

C] By shifting the roller bottom side

D] By shifting the roller upside down

103] What is the type of seed drill?

A] Strip till drill

B] Rubber belt precision seeder

C] Centrifugal seed drill

D] Hand seed drill

104] Which type of speed drill used for sowing of wheat and other cereal crops in already prepared field?

A] Rubber belt precision seeder

B] Strip till drill

C] Zero till drill seed cum fertilizer drill

D] Centrifugal seed drill

105] What is the function of repeller wheel in the cell wheel precision seeder?

A] Removes the super fluous seeds

B] Ensure uniform deliver of seeds

C] Ensure the seeds to fall down at bottom

D] Provide accurate drilling

106] What is the name of seed drill?

A] Centrifugal seed drill

B] Hand seed drill

C] Pneumatic seed drill

D] Strip till drill

107] What is the type of seed drill?

A] Hand seed drill

B] Centrifugal seed drill

C] Pneumatic seed drill

D] Strip till drill

108] Which is the manually operated seed drill?

A] Centrifugal seed drill

B] Pneumatic seed drill

C] Hand seed drill

D] Cell wheel precision seeder

109] What is the function of seed drills?

A] Digging multiple holes for trans planting

B] Drops seeds uniformly without injurry

C] Grading and levelling of fields

D] Breaking the clods

1] Which sprayers are operated usually with Internal Combustion engines?

a) Power sprayer

b) Hydraulic sprayer

c) Commercial sprayer

d) Foot sprayer

2] What is the pressure at which Power sprayers are operated?

a) 68-103 kg/cm2

b) 20-55 kg/cm2

c) 106-141 kg/cm2

d) 120-155 kg/cm2

3] What is the rotating speed of an agitator in a power sprayer?

a) 400-500 rev/min

b) 900-1000 rev/min

c) 600-700 rev/min

d) 100-200 rev/min

4] In which nozzle narrow elliptical spray pattern is formed?

a) Hollow cone nozzle

b) Solid cone nozzle

c) Fan type nozzle

d) Nozzle boss

5] The operating pressure of fan nozzle, which is undesirable is ______

a) 1]2 kg/cm2

b) 1]5 kg/cm2

c) 9 kg/cm2

d) 5]9 kg/cm2

6] Which nozzle covers the entire area at small range?

a) Solid cone nozzle

b) Fan nozzle

c) Hollow cone

d) Nozzle tip

7] Which part of power sprayer is used to prevent corrosion?

a) Agitator

b) Strainer

c) Prime mover

d) Tank

8] Which part of power sprayer is used to break the liquid into desired spray and deliver to plants?

a) Boom

b) Nozzle

c) Strainer

d) Pressure gauge

9] What is rate of the spinning disc, attached to the motor, in Ultra low volume sprayer?

a) 4000-9000
b) 1000-3000
c) 750-1000
d) 10000-15000

10] Who invented world's first self-propelled sprayer?

a) Ray Hagie
b) Elon Musk
c) John Deere
d) Rachel Carson

11] Aldrin is the ________

a) inorganic compound
b) oil compound as spray material
c) organic compound as spray material
d) solution

12] The tank capacity of hydro-pneumatic sprayers, is about ________

a) 1135]5 l
b) 2000 l
c) 750 l
d) 1000 l or less

13] By using a knapsack sprayer, a man can spray over the area of about ________

a) 1 ha per day
b) 0]75 ha per day
c) 1]25 ha per day
d) 0]4 ha per day

14] Who invented duster?

a) H]D] Norman
b) C]E] Ramser
c) Susan Hibbard
d) W]H] Sleeper

15] A tractor sprayer is fitted with 20 hollow cones nozzles to attain application rate of 200 l/hr] During the calibration test, the nozzle flow rate was found to be 1]25 l/min whereas, the rated nozzle flow rate was found to be 0]473 l/min was available at 275 kPa] If the nozzle produces droplets with volume median diameter 200 μm at 1 Mg Pascal, the droplet at the desire flow rate is?

a) 161 μm
b) 164 μm
c) 167 μm
d) 170 μm
1] Power tiller is a ___________
a) Prime mower
b) Orchard mower
c) Small tractor
d) Garden tractor
2] Which of the following country uses more power tiller?
a) India
b) Japan
c) Russia
d) America
3] In India, the introduction of power tiller was in?
a) 1963
b) 1950
c) 1940
d) 1981
4] The kerosene oil operate power is ___________
a) Kubota
b) Krishi
c) Iseski
d) Mitsubishi
5] In power tiller, the power is obtained from ___________
a) I]C] engine
b) Power rim
c) Gasoline
d) Coal
6] In power tiller, the tilling attachment receives the power from _____
a) Main clutch
b) Tilling clutch
c) PTO
d) Transmission gear
7] In bigger power tillers, the type of main clutch used is __________
a) Friction clutch
b) Rubber clutch
c) V-belt clutch

d) Leather clutch

8] In power tillers, the most commonly used brake is ___________

a) Inner side expansion type

b) Friction type

c) Shoe type

d) Rubber plate type

9] In power tiller, the steering clutch lever is possible ___________

a) On the grip of right and left handles

b) On right handle

c) On left handle

d) In front of driver seat

10] Useful life of power tiller is ___________

a) 10 years

b) 15 years

c) 5 years

d) 2 years

11] The HP of ISEKI made power tiller is ___________

a) 8

b) 7

c) 5-7

d) 9

12] In power tiller for transmitting the power from engine to the main clutch the belt used is ___________

a) V-belt

b) Leather belt

c) Canvas belt

d) Flat belt

13] In power tiller, the wheel receives the power from __________

a) Tilting clutch

b) Steering clutch

c) Main clutch

d) PTO

14] In power tiller, the engine transmits the power first to __________

a) Main clutch

b) Wheels

c) Steering clutch

d) Transmission gear

118] Capacitance is not affected by...

A] plate area

B] distance between plates

C] dialectic material

D] frequency

119] The capacitive reactance of a capacitor varies...

A] directly with frequency

B] inversely with frequency

C] directly with applied voltage

D] inversely with applied voltage

120] A capacitor acquired 3 coulombs of charge when 6 volts are applied across it] It has a capacitance of ...

A] 0]5 farad

B] 3 farads

C] 3 farads

D] 18 farads

121] A capacitor is connected across a 200 volt AC line, its minimum voltage rating should be...

A] 100 volts

B] 200 Volts

C] 300 volts

D] 400 volts

122] when testing a capacitor with an ohmmeter, the meter indicates some resistance] The capacitor under test is...

A] leaky

B] open

C] good

D] short

123] The total capacitance of a 40 micro farad capacitor connected in series with an 80 micro farad capacitor is...

A] 26]7 micro farad

B] 40 micro farad

C] 60]6 micro farad

D] 120 micro farad

124] For obtaining 1 micro farad capacitor from 3 nos] of 3 micro farad capacitors we have to connect...

A] all in parallel

B] all in series

C] 2 series and one in parallel

D] none of the above

125] In an AC series circuit having R and C the current flowing through the capacitor will be...

A] lagging the voltage

B] leading the voltage

C] in phase with the voltage

D] none of the above

126] If the frequency of the supply is increased in the R-C series circuit the capacitive reactance will be

A] reduced

B] increased

C] having no effect

D] none of the above

127] Power companies are interested in improving the power factor to

A] reduce line current

B] increase motor efficiency

C] increase volt-amperes

D] decrease power

128] A capacitor increases the power factor value of an AC motor load when it is connected...

A] in series with the motor

B] in series with the starter

C] in parallel with the motor

D] in series with the main winding

129] Normally, the power factor of an incandescent lighting circuit is]]

A] 0

B] 0]5

C] 0]707

D] 1]0

130] When resistance alone is used to determine current in an RLC series circuit, the circuit is...

A] an inductive circuit

B] a capacitive circuit

C] a combination circuit

D] a resonant circuit

131] Inductive reactance is directly related to]]

A] resistance

B] frequency

C] capacitance

D] power

132] Synchronous motor when used for power factor improvement should be...

A] under excited

B] over excited

C] loaded

D] running at no load

133] In a RL parallel circuit, the opposition to total current is called...

A] reactance

B] resistance

C] a vector sum

D] impedance

134] In a AC parallel RL circuit, the power dissipated at the

A] impedance

B] resistance

C] inductance

D] capacitance

1] Mysto hand is a type of which sprayer?

a) Stirrup pump type

b) Hand atomiser type

c) Bucket sprayer

d) Boom type field sprayer

2] Which sprayer is carried on the back of the operator?

a) Knapsack type

b) Stirrup pump type

c) Rocket sprayer

d) Bucket sprayer

3] Vane type or Propeller type are which type of pump?

a) Piston pump

b) Centrifugal pump

c) High volume pump

d) Rotary pump

4] What will be the water power which is required to discharge liquid at the rate of 30 litres/min at 30 kg/cm2 pressure?

a) 2]39 KW

b) 9]86 KW

c) 1]47 KW

d) 2]08 KW

5] Find the suction capacity of a power sprayer if diameter is 25 m, speed is 1100 rev/min length of stroke is 22 mm, number of plunger is 3]

a) 35]61 l/min

b) 23]90 l/min

c) 56]89 l/min

d) 35]47 l/min

6] Hand atomizer is used for spraying in ________

a) orchard

b) field crop

c) nursery

d) forests

7] At where is the pressure lower when the chemical travels through the rubber hose?

a) At the discharge part of the power sprayer

b) At the end of the hose

c) At the swirl plate

d) At the spray gun

8] What is pump efficiency?

a) P]E] = Water Horse Power * Shaft Horse Power

b) P]E] = Water Horse Power – Shaft Horse Power

c) P]E] = Water Horse Power + Shaft Horse Power

d) P]E] = WaterHorsePowerShaftHorsePower

9] The distance from the source water surface to the output of the pump is known as __________

a) total head

b) crank handle

c) nozzle

d) flow rate

10] In a pump, suction volume is 25 litres/min and the pump efficiency is 85%] Calculate the shaft power at a pressure of 35kg/cm2

a) 2]65 KW

b) 3]45 KW

c) 1]67 KW

d) 1]10 KW

110] What is the type of device used in drip irrigation?

A] Disc filter

B] Screen filter

C] Media filter

D] Conical filter

111] What is the advantage of sprinkler irrigation system?

A] Priming not required

B] Chances of air lock remote

C] Efficient use of water

D] Large delivery flow obtained

112] Which type of emergency shut off valve used in irrigation system?

A] Gate valve

B] Pressure release valve

C] Needle valve

D] Check valve

113] What is the purpose of irrigation valve?

A] Supply and control water flow

B] Maintain constant pressure

C] Reduce the water flow

D] Prevent fluid back flow

114] Why the discharge value is closed before stopping the centrifugal pump?

A] Prevent air lock

B] Prevent damage to check value

C] Prevent water hammering

D] Prevent damage to impeller

115] What must be the gap maintained from the bottom and sides during errection of centrifugal pump?

A] 50 cm

B] 60 cm

C] 80 cm

D] 85 cm

116] What is the purpose of diffuser vanes provided in the multi stage pumps?

A] Increase the working pressure

B] Provide uniform distribution of pressure

C] Decrease the working pressure

D] Regulate the fluid flow

117] What is the type of irrigation pump?

A] Single volute

B] Double volute

C] Rotary pump
D] Positive displacement pump
118] What is the result of loss of prime in centrifugal pump?
A] Pressure out put increased
B] Out let pressure decreased
C] <u>Pump may damage</u>
D] Pump produce poor delivery
119] What is the advantage of using centrifugal pump in irrigation?
A] Suction limit is more
B] Priming not required
C] <u>Simple and economical</u>
D] Over loading prevented
120] What is the name of centrifugal pump part?
A] <u>Semi open type impeller</u>
B] Open type impeller
C] Closed type impeller
D] Radial flow impeller
121] What is the typ of irrigation pump?
A] Rotary pump
B] <u>Centrifugal pump</u>
C] Vacuum pump
D] Hydraulic pump
122] Which is the cheapest method of irrigation?
A] Furrow irrigation
B] Drip irrigation
C] Ground water irrigation
D] <u>Flood irrigation</u>
123] Which source of irrigation discharge water with high mineral and elevated temp?
A] Streams
B] Well
C] <u>Springs</u>
D] Lakes
124] Which source of irrigation involves industrial and agriculture waste water?
A] <u>Surface source</u>
B] Streams
C] Lakes

D] Wells

125] What is the advantage of weeding?

A] Ensure deep cultivation

B] Ensure shallow cultivation

C] Purity of seed can be maintained

D] Reduction of time consumption

1] Tank of hydraulic sprayers is made of ________

a) Metal

b) Fibre glass

c) Polythene

d) PVC

2] In tank of hydraulic sprayer, the function of drain plug is to _______

a) Regulate the sprayer rate

b) Control the pressure

c) Drain and clean the tank

d) Control volume

3] The kind of agitator used in hydraulic sprayer is ________

a) Paddle type

b) Plunger type

c) Wooden type

d) Glass type

4] In hydraulic sprayer, the air chamber is provided on _________

a) Top of the tank

b) Discharge line of pump

c) Below tank

d) A frame near operator seat

5] In hydraulic sprayers, the pressure gauge is equipped __________

a) On top of the tank

b) On a frame near tank

c) On discharge line of sprayer

d) Below tank

6] In hydraulic sprayer, the cut off valve is used to control the _________

a) Flow to boom

b) Pressure

c) Spray rate

d) Drop size

7] In hydraulic sprayer, the strainer is equipped in _______

a) Delivery line
b) Suction line
c) Boom
d) Tank

8] Most of the hydraulic sprayers are equipped with ________
a) Positive displacement pump
b) Reciprocating pump
c) Centrifugal pump
d) Rotary pump

9] In hydraulic sprayers, the most common length of boom for general field use is _______
a) 16]50 m
b) 15 m
c) 10 m
d) 6]30 m

10] In hydraulic sprayers, the amount of vertical adjustment for spraying on plants of various heights varies from _______
a) 45]7 cm 118 m
b) 20-25 m
c) 1]5 cm to 3]5 m
d) 10-100 m

126] Which type of oil grade to be used for main clutch lever, steering clutch lever of power tiller?
A] SAE 20 - 30
B] SAE 80 - 90
C] SAE 50 - 60
D] SAE 40 - 60

127] What is the speed range of power tillers in general?
A] 4-6 forward speed 1-2 backward speed
B] 4-6 backward speed 1-2 forward speed
C] 2-8 forward speed 4-8 backward speed
D] 4-8 forward speed 2-8 forward speed

128] Which type of engine fitted with power tiller?
A] Petrol engine
B] Diesel engine
C] Steam engine
D] Marine engine

129] What is the horse power range generally used in power tiller?

A] 4]5 Hp to 12 Hp
B] 5 Hp to 10 Hp
C] 2 Hp to 8 Hp
D] 5 Hp to 14 Hp

130] Which type of weeder suitable for loamy and sandy soils?
A] Star type
B] Peg type
C] Power type
D] Rotary type

131] What is the recommended gear position for parking, storage and while starting of weeder?
A] Low 1st
B] Low 2nd
C] Low - Neutral
D] Low reverse

132] What is the type of weeder?
A] Star type weeder
B] Peg tooth weeder
C] Power weeder
D] Rotary type weeder

133] What is the type of weeder?
A] Star type weeder
B] Peg type weeder
C] Power type weeder
D] Rotary type weeder

134] Which tilling method can be applied to irregular field?
A] Return tilling method
B] Circular travel tilling method
C] Place tilling method
D] Alternate tilling method

135] What is the frequency of lubrication oil change in the gear box of power tiller?
A] 5000 Hrs
B] 500 Hrs
C] 1000 Hrs
D] 1500 Hrs

136] What is the type of servicing carried out in AC motor?
A] Replacing bearing

B] Lubricating bearing
C] Cleaning the bearing
D] Greasing the bearing
137] What is the name of device?
A] Squirrel cage motor
B] Bearing puller
C] D]O]L]Starter
D] Starter motor mounting
138] What is the type of crop protection equipment?
A] Sprayer
B] Digger
C] Power duster
D] Harvester
139] What is the formula used to calculate spray application rate?
A] Ltrs / (hrs x area)
B] Hrs / (Ltrs x area)
C] Area/ (Hrs x Litrs)
D] (Ltrs x area)/ Hrs
140] What is the type of sprayer?
A] Knapsack sprayer
B] Foot sprayer
C] Bucket sprayer
D] Rocker sprayer
141] Which sprayer operated by own power unit?
A] Knapsack sprayer
B] Bucket sprayer
C] Self propelled sprayer
D] Rocker sprayer
142] What is the type of sprayer?
A] Bucket sprayer
B] Rocker sprayer
C] Self-propelled sprayer
D] Foot sprayer
143] How to avoid undue pressure an bearings of rotor while servicing AC squirrel cage motor?
A] Hold by hand
B] Hold by vice
C] Hold by clamp

D] Hold by jack

144] How the hydraulic pump is held in the bucket sprayer?

A] By foot rest

B] By pump barrel

C] By pump handle

D] By plat form

145] What is the recommended percentage of grease packing in the races of bearings of AC motors by the manufacture?

A] 75%

B] 80%

C] 65%

D] 90%

146] What is to be checked in the winding of AC motor during servicing?

A] Check dry solder, and insulation

B] Check the grease between winding

C] Check the thickness of winding

D] Check the water presence in winding

147] Why the realignment of shaft position is necessary for rotor during AC motor servicing?

A] Due to damaged insulation

B] Due to dry solder

C] Rotor found locked

D] Inadequate lubrication

148] Which instrument used to check the actual speed of rotor in the D]O]L starter?

A] Manometer

B] Tachometer

C] Hydrometer

D] Voltmeter

149] What is the cause of motor fails to start?

A] Defective bearing

B] Low voltage

C] Excessively loaded

D] Incorrect size of bearing

150] What causes motor starts but does not share load?

A] Low frequency

B] Low voltage

C] Open circuit stator

D] Bearing stiff

151] What will be the effect of incorrect size of fuses in the induction motor?

A] Overheating of the motor

B] Motor fails to star

C] Motor blows off fuses

D] Motor starts but does not share load

152] What is the purpose of agitator provided in the knapsack sprayer?

A] Increase the velocity

B] Ensure uniform spray

C] Prevent the particle in suspension to settle down

D] Filter the dust in the liquid

153] What is the purpose of duster?

A] Increase crop production

B] Control insects in the crop

C] Control mosquito

D] Control weeding

154] Which type of nozzle used for insecticide in the duster?

A] Cut type

B] Needle type

C] Cone type

D] Conical type

155] What is the purpose cut type nozzle used in duster?

A] For wedicides

B] For insecticide

C] For mosquito

D] For fertilizer

156] Which type of sprayer used for small and large scale spraying on field crops?

A] Bucket sprayer

B] Rocker sprayer

C] Power operated sprayer

D] Bettery operated sprayer

157] How the tractor mounted sprayer gets drive?

A] P]T]O shaft of engine

B] Clutch shaft

C] Cam shaft

D] Fly wheel
158] Whate is the material used to make cutter bar of reaper?
A] Mild steel
B] Cast iron
C] High grade steel
D] Medium carbon steel
159] Which device used for manual harvesting crop?
A] Sickle
B] Reaper
C] Mower
D] Combine
160] What is the device used in reaper cum binder?
A] Cage wheel
B] Feeding chute
C] Crop dividers
D] Cutter bar
161] What is the type of thresher?
A] Paddy thresher
B] Ground nut thresher
C] Maize thresher
D] Sunflower thresher
162] What is the name of thresher?
A] Sunflower thresher
B] Ground nut thresher
C] Maize thresher
D] Paddy thresher
163] What is the type of thresher?
A] Paddy thresher
B] Multi crop thresher
C] Sunflower thresher
D] Ground nut thresher
164] What is the type of agriculture equipment?
A] One row potato digger
B] Ground nut digger
C] Agriculture reaper
D] Combine harvester
165] What is the name of agriculture equipment?
A] Potato digger

B] Ground nut digger
C] Rotary harvester
D] Combine harvester
166] What is the name of device?
A] Bat type tyue
B] Combined bat and time type
C] Feeder conveyer
D] Pickup type reel
167] What is the name of combine harvester part?
A] Angle bar cylinder
B] Rasp bar cylinder
C] Rear beater
D] Spike tooth cylinder
168] What is the name of device used in combine harvester?
A] Feed conveyer
B] Wobble plate
C] Auger
D] Pickup type reel
169] What is the capacity of bellow duster container?
A] 2]5 kg to 5]0 kg
B] 1 kg to 3]2 kg
C] 30 g to 500 g
D] 780 g to 900 g
170] What are the combination of combine harvester?
A] Reaper, Duster, Sprayer
B] Reaper, thresher, winnower
C] Digger,thresher, sprayer
D] Auger, digger, reaper
171] What is the type of cylinder used in combine harvester?
A] Spike tooth
B] Angle bar
C] Rasp/ bar cylinder
D] Concave tooth
172] What is the type of thresher?
A] Paddy thresher
B] Maize thresher
C] Axial flow ground nut thresher
D] Vegetable thresher

173] What is the reason for increasing total grain losses in combine harvester?

A] Decrease in forward speed

B] Decrease in stubble height

C] Decrease in concave clearance

D] More moisture content in the crops

174] What is the main function of combine harvester?

A] Threshing

B] Tilling

C] Deep cultivation

D] Weeding

175] Which machine is used for cutting cereal crops?

A] Reaper

B] Combine

C] Mower

D] Windrower

176] What is the name of material left by the harvesting machine in row?

A] Swath

B] Stubble

C] Straw

D] Combine

177] What is alignment in the functioning of reaper?

A] Cutter bar must be in horizontal plane

B] Cutter bar and pitman must be in same vertical plane

C] Pitman must be in vertical plane

D] Cutter bar must be in vertical plane

178] What are the two adjustments for proper functioning of reaper?

A] Registration, alignment

B] Registration, allowance

C] Alignment, clearance

D] Clearance, allowance

179] When the thresher causes more seed damage?

A] Speed increased

B] Clearance increased

C] Feed rate is reduced

D] Speed is reduced

180] What is the optimum moisture content of crop for better threshing?

A] 5 - 10 %

B] 12 - 15 %

C] 15 - 20 %

D] 20 - 30 %

181] How to rectify the defect of broken grains in the thresher?

A] Reduce speed and adjust clearance

B] Increase the speed and adjust clearance

C] Use only dried crops

D] Clean upper sieve

182] How to rectify the broken grain defect in harvester?

A] Increase cylinder speed

B] Decrease clearance between cylindrical concave

C] Reduce cylinder speed

D] Increase the cutting speed

183] Which type of thresher is provided with well balanced cylinder and threshing teeth fixed on wooden slots?

A] Sunflower thresher

B] Paddy thresher

C] Multi crop thresher

D] Maize thresher

184] What is the dia of rotating screen mesh drum in the axial flow vegetable threshers?

A] 1]5 to 1]7 mtrs

B] 1]8 to 2]2 mtrs

C] 1]7 to 2]2 mtrs

D] 1]6 to 1]9 mtrs

185] How to overcome the defect of too many unthreshed heads?

A] Increase concave clearance

B] Decrease concave clearance

C] Decrease drum speed

D] Clean upper sieve

186] What will be the effect of low fan speed in the function of threshers?

A] Grain with tailings

B] Vibration in thresher

C] Straw comes along with grain

D] Grains gets broken

187] How to rectify the defect of grain blows with straw in the thresher?

A] Increase the fan speed

B] Increase the drum speed

C] Use properly dried crop

D] Clean the sieve holes

188] What causes blockage of the drum of thresher?

A] High speed of drum

B] High fan speed

C] Crop is moist

D] Less concave clearance

189] What is the function auger in the cutting system of combine harvester?

A] Collect the chaff mixture

B] Takes the crop from cutter bar

C] Pull the cut crop to the middle of trough

D] Carry the empty straw to the floor

190] Where the straw walkers are mounted in the combine harvester?

A] Cam shaft

B] Crank shaft

C] Clutch shaft

D] On cylinder head

191] What is the advantage of combine harvester?

A] Saves cost of harvesting and threshing

B] Lower initial cost

C] Reduce un employment

D] Maintenance is easy

192] What is the drum speed for wheat crop in combine harvester?

A] 900 - 1000 rpm

B] 800 - 1200 rpm

C] 1200 - 1500 rpm

D] 1150 - 1450 rpm

193] Which type of cylinder used in combine harvester for wheat crop?

A] Spike tooth cylinder

B] Angle bar cylinder

C] Resp/ bar cylinder

D] Concave toothed cylinder

194] What will be the effect of sudden replenishing of cooling water due to rise in engine temp in the combine harvester?

A] Cylinder head and cylinder block may crack

B] Engine temperature will fall down

C] Engine performance improved

D] Lubrication function improved

195] Which type of cylinder only used for rice or soya bean in the combine harvester?

A] Rasp bar

B] Spike tooth

C] Angle bar

D] Concave type

196] What is the main function of winnower?

A] Remove the dust from grain

B] Separate the grain from chaff

C] Threshing of crops

D] Bring the cut crops to middle

197] Which tool used to dismantle the cage wheel from reaper?

A] Pin wrench

B] Spanner

C] Chisel and Hammer

D] Common screw driver

198] What is the name of harvesting equipment?

A] Rectangular baler

B] Hydraulic tipping trailer

C] HUSK separater

D] Straw hay raker

199] What is the type of equipment?

A] Power chaff cutter

B] Mannual chaff cutter

C] Pneumatic chaff cutter

D] Mechanical chaff cutter

200] What is the name of part marked as X in the motor driven direct coupled hammer mill?

A] Screen

B] Shaft

C] Metal trap

D] Wear plate

201] What is the name of agriculture equipment?

A] Pottato digger

B] Hammer mill

C] Ground nut digger

D] Combine harvester

202] What is the type of force indicated in the schematic diagram?

A] Compressive

B] Attrition

C] Impact

D] Cut

203] Which type of force indicated in the schematic diagram?

A] Cut

B] Compressive

C] Impact

D] Attrition

204] Which storage structure is made of mud or bricks with a polythene film embedded within the walls?

A] Pusa bin

B] PAV bin

C] Hapur tekka

D] Silos

205] Which equipment used for the application of cutting force in the hammer mill function?

A] Rotary knife cutter

B] Disc attrition mill

C] Hammer mill

D] Crusing rolls

206] Which equipment is used for NUTCRACKER?

A] Hammer mill

B] Scissorrs

C] Crushing rolls

D] File

207] What is the basic function of hammer mill?

A] Produce larger particle from smaller one

B] Produce smaller particle from larger one

C] Clean the grain surface

D] Remove chaff of grains

208] What is the purpose of rice huller?

A] Cleans the field faster

B] Separate the grain from stalks

C] Remove chaff of grains of rice

D] Clean the grain

209] What is the advantage of underground storage?

A] Safe from threats such as theft, rain, wind

B] Dispatched without difficulty

C] Easier to load or un load

D] Sweating of grain does not arise

210] Which small scale storage structure provided with galvanised metal iron structure?

A] Pusa bin

B] PAU bin

C] Hapur tekka

D] Silos

211] What is the name of rice huller component?

A] Bran remover

B] Rubber roll paddy husker

C] HUSK aspirator with rubber roll husker

D] Dehusker

212] What is the name of part marked as X in the hammer mill?

A] Rotor

B] Hammer

C] Discharge pipe

D] Fan

213] What is the type of post harvesting equipment?

A] Crushing rolls

B] Disc attrition mill

C] Direct coupled hammer mill

D] Rotary knife cutter

214] What is the use of destoner?

A] Separate stones from the rice grain

B] Remove the paddy husk

C] Separate husk

D] Remove immature grains

215] What is the advantage of rubber roll paddy husker in the rice huller?

A] Polishing the grain

B] Reduce grain breakage

C] Remove bran layer from grain

D] Separate broken grain

216] Which is the common drying method used to pressure the root products in tropical countries? A] Sun drying method

B] Hot air drying method

C] Artificial solar driers

D] Vaccum drying method

217] What is the purpose of hammer mill?

A] Removing the weed

B] Reduce the size of soild material

C] Cutting straw or hay

D] Digging out ground nut

218] Which type of force used in hammer mill?

A] Impact

B] Compressive

C] Attrition

D] Cut

219] Who is responsible to maintain the operator mannual?

A] Operator

B] Workshop in charge

C] Owner of equipment

D] Customer

220] Which type of combine harvester have separate engine connected with tractor?

A] Self-propelled harvesting combines

B] Pulled type with auxiliary engine

C] Pull type harvesting combines

D] Semi propelled harvesting combines

221] What is the storage capacity of silos?

A] 20000 tons

B] 15000 tons

C] 25000 tons

D] 30000 tons

222] Which storage structure is economic on large scale?

A] PAU bin

B] Silos

C] CAP storage

D] Pusa bin

223] Where you will find the vehicle registration number in the form record keeping?

A] Log book

B] Service mannual

C] Operation mannual

D] Manufacturer mannual

224] What is the purpose of puddling?

A] Conservation of soil moisture

B] Purity of seed maintained

C] Tilling the paddy field

D] Used for drip irrigation

225] Which type of tilling method is used to wet-soft paddy field?

A] Return tilling method

B] Circular travel tilling method

C] Alternate tilling method

D] Continuous tilling method

226] Where the control levers and switches are located in the power tiller?

A] Near handle

B] On the chasis

C] Near the engine mounting

D] Near intake system

227] What is the effect of main clutch lever in power tiller moved to "off" position?

A] Driving power cut off from engine

B] Speed change lever come to "Neutral"

C] Brake operating lever will not move

D] Rotary speed change lever move to low speed

228] What is the function of reel in combine harvester?

A] Purpose corps toward cutter

B] Picks up loose hay

C] To spread the cut hay

D] Reduce the size of solid materials

229] Which is the requirement of ideal grain storage structure?

A] It should be economical

B] It should be shock proof

C] It should be water and moisture proof

D] It should with stand temperature variation

INDUSTRIAL TRAINING INSTITUTE

Monthly Test-1, Marks- 20, Date:- ______________

(Every Question Carry Two Marks)

52] Which power system drives post hole digger?

A] Hydraulic system

B] Pneumatic system

C] Mechanical system

D] Electrical system

53] What is the use of post hole digger?

A] Dig multiple holes for fence posts

B] Deep cultivation

C] Tilling the soil between row corps

D] Grading and levelling of fields

54] What is the name of agriculture implement?

A] Scraper

B] Pest hole digger

C] Cultivator

D] Dumper

55] Which agriculture equipment used for rough levelling and cutting of high spots?

A] Scraper

B] Dumper

C] Leveller

D] Digger

56] What is the use of scraper?

A] Loading and unloading soil from one place to other

B] Deep cultivation

C] Tilling the soil between row corps

D] Prepare the land by breaking clods

57] What is the type of agriculture implement?

A] Scraper

B] Dumper

C] Leveller

D] Cultivator

1] In which process of seeding, the seeds are placed in the holes made in seed bed and covering them?

a) Broadcasting

b) Transplanting

c) Dibbling

d) Drilling

2] Which of the following is not a type of Drilling?

a) Sowing behind the plough

b) Bullock drawn seed drills

c) Tractor drawn seed drills

d) Check row planting

3] In which seed metering mechanism, the feed wheel is provided with fine and coarse ribbed flanges?

a) Internal double run type

b) Fluted feed type

c) Cell feed mechanism

d) Brush feed mechanism

4] Calculate the cost of seeding one hectare of land with bullock-drawn seed drill of 5*22 cm size] The speed of bullocks is 3km/hr] Hire charges of bullocks ? 100/- per pair, hire charges of seed drill is ? 50/- per day and wage of operator ? 100/- per day of 8 hours]

a) ? 84]88

b) ? 94]68

c) ? 110]90

d) ? 34]29

INDUSTRIAL TRAINING INSTITUTE

Monthly Test-2, Marks- 20, Date:- ______________

(Every Question Carry Two Marks)

5] A fluted feed seed drill has eight furrow openers of single disc type] The furrow openers are spaced 25 cm apart and the main drive wheel has a diameter of 120 cm] How many turns of main drive wheel would occur when the seed drill has covered one hectare of area?

a) 1333]3

b) 1666]6

c) 1999]9

d) 1234]5

6] Calculate the time required for sowing 1]6 hectares of land by five furrows seed drill going 12]5 cm deep] The speed of seed drill is 3]2 km/hr and pressure exerted by the soil on the seed drill is 0]42 kg/cm2] The space between furrow openers is 10 cm and loss in turning is 10%]

a) 21]07 hrs

b) 9]87 hrs
c) 2]34 hrs
d) 11]11 hrs

7] Calculate the seed rate/hectare of a 7*17 cm seed drill, whose main drive wheel is 124 cm diameter and total weight of grain collected in 20 revolutions in 0]423 kg]

a) 45]58 kg
b) 54]34 kg
c) 90 kg
d) 23]78 kg

8] Maximum yield of maize is obtained with a population of 40000 plants per hectare] The rows are 140cm apart and an average emergence of 85% is expected] How many seeds per hill should be planted if hills are 140cm apart?

a) 9
b) 2
c) 10
d) 11

9] Which seed metering mechanism consists of cups of spoon on the periphery of a vertical rotating disc?

a) Cup feed mechanism
b) Cell feed mechanism
c) Brush feed mechanism
d) Picker wheel mechanism

10] Which seeding method uses Malobansa?

a) Transplanting
b) Seed dropping behind the plough
c) Check row planting
d) Hill dropping

1] Which of the following is not a type of furrow opener?

a) Shovel type
b) Shoe type
c) Disc type
d) Brush feed type

58] What is the material used to make the blade of leveller?

A] High carbon steel
B] Medium carbon steel
C] Low carbon steel

D] Stain less steel

59] Which agriculture equipment used for uniform distribution of water in the field?

A] Scraper

B] Dumper

C] Leveller

D] Tiller

60] What is the name of soil forming equipment?

A] Dumper

B] Leveller

C] Scraper

D] Hole digger

INDUSTRIAL TRAINING INSTITUTE

Monthly Test-3, Marks- 20, Date:- _______________

(Every Question Carry Two Marks)

61] What is the use of trenchers?

A] Laying pipes and making tunnels

B] Deep cultivation

C] Loading and unloading of soil

D] Clean the mud from auger

62] What is the periodical oil change in the gear box unit and transmission unit of ditcher?

A] 30 Hrs

B] 50 Hrs

C] 60 Hrs

D] 80 Hrs

63] What is the type of furrow opener?

A] Single disc opener

B] Double Disc type

C] Hoe type

D] Shoe type

64] What is the purpose of furrow opener?

A] Used to store the seed in machine

B] Open a furrow in the soil at uniform depth

C] Used for deep cultivation

D] Uniform spreading of seeds

65] Which part of fertilizer applicator ensures High degree of uniforming in sowing?

A] Spiral tubes
B] Rubber tubes
C] Polythene tubes
D] Telescopic tubes

66] What is the advantage of using polythene or rubber tubes in the fertilizer applicator?
A] Clogging and choking easily detectable
B] Flexibility in usage
C] Easy Handling
D] Reduction of weight

67] what is the advantage of serrated disc in the fertilizer applicator?
A] Prevent the gravitational flow fertilizer
B] Maintain the constant speed
C] Crushing the small clods of fertilizer
D] Provide uniform spreading of fertilizer

68] What is the name of device in fetilizer applicator?
A] Spur wheel
B] Ground wheel
C] Star wheel
D] Serrated disc

69] Why the spur wheel of fertilizer applicator width is more than the notch?
A] Prevent gravitation flow of fertilizer at rest
B] Provide uniform flow of fertilizer
C] prevent stucking of spur wheel
D] Increase the speed of spur wheel

70] What is the material used to make spur wheel of fetilizer metering device?
A] Castiron
B] High carbon steel
C] Aluminium casting
D] stainless steel

INDUSTRIAL TRAINING INSTITUTE

Monthly Test-4, Marks- 20, Date:- ______________

(Every Question Carry Two Marks)

2] Which of the following is not a type of a Shovel?
a) Reversible
b) Spear point

c) Reciprocating power

d) Single point

3] What is the minimum carbon content and thickness of Shoe type furrow?

a) 0]5% and 4mm

b) 0]5% and 2mm

c) 0]2% and 4mm

d) 0]8% and 8mm

4] What is the minimum diameter of seed and fertilizer tube in disc type furrow opener?

a) 30mm

b) 45mm

c) 60mm

d) 25mm

5] Which furrow opener has toe and 'T' shaped scrapers?

a) Reversible shovel

b) Double disc type

c) Spear point shovel

d) Single disc type

6] What is the range of the implement used in cultivator with seeding attachment?

a) 600-700mm

b) 400-500mm

c) 100-200mm

d) 900-1000mm

7] Which seed metering device mechanism in a planter brushes out excess seeds from the cells of the feed mechanism?

a) Edge drop

b) Cut off

c) Knock out

d) Flat drop

8] What is the field capacity of a potato planter (semi-automatic)?

a) 0]15-0]25 ha/hr

b) 0]10-0]14 ha/hr

c) 0]40-0]55 ha/hr

d) 0]09-0]14 ha/hr

9] Which planter has six C-type blades on its flanges?

a) Potato planter

b) Low land paddy seeder
c) Rice trans planter
d) Zero till drill
10] What is the capacity of potato planter (Automatic)?
a) 1000-4000 potatoes/hour
b) 200-900 potatoes/hour
c) 6000-14000 potatoes/hour
d) 16000-32000 potatoes/hour
1] At what height should the transplanting be done in paddy?
a) 5-10 cm
b) 15-20 cm
c) 45-50 cm
d) 30-35 cm

INDUSTRIAL TRAINING INSTITUTE

Monthly Test-5, Marks- 20, Date:- ______________

(Every Question Carry Two Marks)

2] What should be the spacing of paddy in the sub-normal conditions?
a) 15*10 cm2
b) 24*12 cm2
c) 34*24 cm2
d) 8*12 cm2
71] What is the name of agriculture implement?
A] Fertilizer Applicator
B] Marking roller
C] Automatic planter
D] Sugarcane planter
72] Which is the essential factor of fertilizer applicator?
A] Application rate should be adjustable
B] Application speed should be constant
C] Fertilizer applicator should be simple in construction
D] Easy replacement of defective parts
73] Why furrow opener becomes heavy and accumulated with seed and soil in the planter?
A] Fertilizer not properly metered
B] Improper sowing rate
C] Improper seed bed preparation
D] Dis placement of seed

74] What will be the effect in reverse operation of vegetable transplanter?

A] Furrow opener will be bend

B] Furrow opener will be filled with soil

C] Furrow opener will break

D] Displacement of seed in the furrow

75] What is the formula used to calculate sowing rate?

A] Kg seed per ha=(D x W)/P

B] Kg seed per ha=(D +W)/P

C] Kg seed per ha=(D - W)/P

D] Kg seed per ha=(W - D)/P

76] Which planting allows the soil to dry rapidly and gaurds againts excess moisture?

A] Flat planting

B] Bed planting

C] Furrows planting

D] Blisters planting

77] Which crop is suitable for ridge planting?

A] Maize

B] Cotton

C] sugarcane

D] Potato

78] Which method of planting followed for maize crops?

A] Flat land planting

B] Ridge planting

C] Furrow planting

D] Vertical land planting

79] What is the speed of sugarcane planter?

A] 0]4 - 4 km/hr

B] 0]8 - 5 km/hr

C] 0]6 - 7 km/hr

D] 0]5 - 5 km/hr

INDUSTRIAL TRAINING INSTITUTE

Monthly Test-6, Marks- 20, Date:- ______________

(Every Question Carry Two Marks)

80] What is the row spacing of rice crops?

A] 20 x 10 cm

B] 25 x 15 cm

C] 20 x 20 cm

D] 25 x 20 cm

81] What is the name of planter?

A] Corn planter

B] Potato planter

C] Paddy planter

D] Vegetable trans planter

82] What is the purpose of inclined press wheels in the vegetable trans planter?

A] Spacing the trans plantation

B] Firm soil around the root

C] Maintain the depth of plant

D] Changing the planting depth

83] What is the spacing distance between the rows to be maintained in power tiller mounted rice planting?

A] 10 cm

B] 15 cm

C] 20 cm

D] 25 cm

84] How the tray movement mechanism achived in the manual paddy trans planting?

A] By worm gear and shaft

B] By chain and free wheel

C] By wheel and shaft

D] By rack and pinion

85] What is the name of planter?

A] Sugarcane planter

B] cotton planter

C] Potato planter

D] Two row multi crop planter

3] Which geometry has smothering effect on weeds?

a) Planting

b) Triangular

c) Circular

d) Square

4] How many seedlings per hill is recommended to transplant?

a) 6-7

b) 7-8

c) 2-3

d) 5-6

5] What should be the transplanting depth of paddy?

a) 2-3 cm

b) 4-5 cm

c) 8-9 cm

d) 6-7 cm

6] In which country the rice trans planters were developed?

a) India

b) Pakistan

c) China

d) Japan

INDUSTRIAL TRAINING INSTITUTE

Monthly Test-7, Marks- 20, Date:- _____________

(Every Question Carry Two Marks)

7] Which part of the rice trans planter acts like a shed roof to the seedlings?

a) Seedling tray

b) Motor

c) Running gear

d) Gear box

8] The accuracy of the planter does not depend on ________

a) Speed of seed plate

b) Shape of hopper bottom

c) Uniformity of seed size

d) Weather

1] Which part operates the tractor drawn semi-mounted or mounted type mowers?

a) PTO shaft

b) Cutter

c) Pitman

d) Grass board

2] Which clutch is used in the driving unit of a mower?

a) Fluid coupling

b) Dog clutch

c) Friction clutch

d) Single plate

3] What is the difference between each knife clips?

a) 5-15 cm
b) 40-50 cm
c) 35-45 cm
d) 20-30 cm

4] When the knife section stops in the centre of its guard on every stroke, it is known as?

a) Re-embankment
b) Reinforcement
c) Registration
d) Rescue

5] Calculate the total time required to harvest 2]5 hectares of grass by means of a 2 metre mower being operated at 4 km/hr] (Field efficiency=80%)

a) 2]5 hrs
b) 1]2 hrs
c) 3]9 hrs
d) 7 hrs

6] What power is required to pull 1]2 mete mower working at a speed of 4]8 km/hr, if there is a load of 50 kg per metre length of mower and mechanical efficiency is 80%?

a) 1 KW
b) 0]98 KW
c) 0]23 KW
d) 2 KW

7] How many hectares per day of 10 hours can be cut by a combine with 4 metre cutter bar, when it is running at 4 k/hr?

a) 16ha
b) 20 ha
c) 28 ha
d) 8 ha

8] A mower has drive wheel of 60 cm diameter] The crank of the mower makes 600 rev/min when it is driven by a tractor, moving at a speed of 2]3 km/hr] If the speed ratio between the crank wheel and land wheel is changed to 27:1, calculate the increase in speed of mower to maintain same speed of crank]

a) 0]19 km/hr
b) 0]67 km/hr
c) 0]11 km/hr

d) 0]21 km/hr

INDUSTRIAL TRAINING INSTITUTE

Monthly Test-8, Marks- 20, Date:- ____________

(Every Question Carry Two Marks)

9] Which part of mower is used to regulate the height of cut above the ground?

a) Ledger plate

b) Wearing plate

c) Shoe

d) Grass board

86] What is the type of planter?

A] Potato planter

B] Semi automatic planter

C] sugarcane planter

D] Cotton planter

87] How the spacing of seed is achieved in the semi automatic planter?

A] By changing the running wheel

B] By changing the feed ring

C] By adjusting furrow opener

D] By changing the direction of conveyer belt

88] What is the name of planter?

A] Two row multi crop planter

B] Three row multi crop planter

C] Automatic planter

D] Cotton planter

89] How many picker arms are attached with picker wheel of potato planter?

A] 12 Nos

B] 10 Nos

C] 8 Nos

D] 6 Nos

90] What is the type of planter?

A] Potato planter

B] Three row multi crop planter

C] Sugarcane planter

D] Two row multicrop planter

91] What is the cause of excessive vibration in the machine of happy seeder?

A] Broken flail blades
B] PTO shaft not engaging
C] Seed / fertilizer box empty
D] Fertilizer fluted roller is blocked

92] How much chloropyrophos to be added with seed to protect against termite attack in the happy seeder?
A] 2 ml / kg of seed
B] 3 ml / kg of seed
C] 4 ml / kg of seed
D] 5 ml / kg of seed

93] Which part of happy seeder regulate insertion of the furrow openers in to the soil to place seed at desired depth?
A] Drive wheel
B] Two depth control wheels
C] P]T]O shaft
D] Flail shaft

94] Where the fertilizwer box is mounted in the happy seeder?
A] Front side of frame
B] rear side of frame
C] Near the flail shaft
D] Top of frame

INDUSTRIAL TRAINING INSTITUTE
Monthly Test-9, Marks- 20, Date:- ______________
(Every Question Carry Two Marks)

95] What is the purpose flail blades of furrow opener in the happy seeder?
A] Clean the furrow opener
B] Sharpen the tynes
C] Deliver the seed uniformly
D] Deliver the fertilizer evenly

96] What is the function of furrow opener in happy seeder?
A] Drill and place seed and fertilizer
B] Spread combine harvested rice straw
C] Control fertilizer application
D] Store the seed in the machine

97] Which agricultural implement combines stubble mulching and seed drilling in to one machine?
A] Cultivator

B] Happy seeder

C] Hand seed drill

D] Rotavator

98] Which type of seed & fertilizer device is used in drills for crops where seeds are easily damaged due to rough mechanical handling?

A] Cup type

B] Hoe type

C] Stub runner type

D] Full runner type

99] What is the provision is made for different sizes of seeds in the metering device?

A] Adjustable spring loaded baffle plate

B] Fluted rollar

C] Longitudinal grooves

D] Square shaft

1] Calculate the total time required to harvest 4 hectares of grass by means of a 2mm mower being operated at the speed of 4 km/h] Assume field efficiency of mower as 75%?

a) 4]67 hr

b) 5]67 hr

c) 6]67 hr

d) 7]67 hr

2] What horsepower will be required to pull 1]2 m mower working at the speed of 5 km/m length of the mower ad mechanical efficiency is 85%?

a) 1]56

b) 2]56

c) 3]56

d) 4]56

3] How many hectares of grass per day of 15 hours can be cut by a mower being operated at the speed of 4]5 km/h and with 4 m cutter bar]

a) 20

b) 22

c) 27

d) 16

4] A mower has driven wheel of 60 cm diameter] The crank of mower makes 550 rpm, when it is driven by a tractor at a speed of 2 km/h] If speed ratio between the crank wheel and land wheel is changed to 27:1, calculate the increase in speed of mower to maintain the same speed of crank]

a) 0]20 km/h
b) 0]304 km/h
c) 1]402 km/h
d) 1]36 km/h

5] A 2m mower is operating at 3]5 km/h with an overall efficiency of 75%] Calculate the area covered by it in ha/h]

a) 0]525
b) 0]625
c) 0]725
d) 0]825

INDUSTRIAL TRAINING INSTITUTE

Monthly Test-10, Marks- 20, Date:- ______________

(Every Question Carry Two Marks)

6] How many revolutions will each spindle of cotton picker make in the picking zone for a chain belt arrangement in which the speed of spindle is 1400 rpm and remains in the picking zone during 100 cm of forward travel]

a) 50
b) 21
c) 45
d) 11

7] A disc type mower is operated by PTO with 6 discs with a shaft of 0]4 m/disc] The specific energy required for cutting is 2]1 KJ/m2 and specific power losses due to air come stubble and gear train friction is 2 kw/m of cutting width] If the mower with tractor requires a propelling force of 2 KN the total power requirement for carrying out moving in Kw at forward speed of 3 km/h is ____

a) 10]67
b) 20]67
c) 30]67
d) 40]67

8] The most common mower, amongst the following is ____________

a) Reciprocating mower
b) Lawn mower
c) Cylindrical mower
d) Horizontal mower

9] A gang mower is the group of ____________

a) 2 or more cylindrical mowers
b) 5 mowers

c) 2 mowers
d) 10 mowers
10] In flail mower, the cutting section contains ___________
a) Cutter bar
b) Swinging knives
c) Fixed knives
d) Reciprocating fingers only
11] In cutter bar of mower, the knife head is attached to the ___________
a) Knife back
b) Cutter end
c) Starting point of cutting edge
d) Reciprocating fingers
12] In mower, the grass board is provided at the ___________
a) Cutter end
b) Knife end
c) Knife back
d) Reciprocating fingers
13] In cutter bar of mower, the knife sections are revitted to the ___________
a) Knife back
b) Reciprocating fingers
c) Stationary bar
d) Cylindrical drum
14] In mower, the pitman transmits the motion to the ___________
a) Knife head
b) Knife middle
c) Knife back
d) Knife end
15] Who invented the first lawn mower?
a) Albert Einstein
b) Buzz Aldrin
c) Edwin Budding
d) Yuri Gagarin

INDUSTRIAL TRAINING INSTITUTE

Monthly Test-11, Marks- 20, Date:- ______________

(Every Question Carry Two Marks)

100] What is the type of seed & fertilizer metering device?

A] Fluted feed type

B] Cup type

C] Interuce double rum type

D] Sub rummer type

101] What is the type of seed drill?

A] Rubber belt precision seeder

B] Hand seed drill

C] Zero till drill seed cum fertilizer drill

D] Pneumatic seed drill

102] How the amount of seed sown is changed in seed cum fertilizer drill?

A] By shifting the roller sideways

B] By shifting the roller upper side

C] By shifting the roller bottom side

D] By shifting the roller upside down

103] What is the type of seed drill?

A] Strip till drill

B] Rubber belt precision seeder

C] Centrifugal seed drill

D] Hand seed drill

104] Which type of speed drill used for sowing of wheat and other cereal crops in already prepared field?

A] Rubber belt precision seeder

B] Strip till drill

C] Zero till drill seed cum fertilizer drill

D] Centrifugal seed drill

105] What is the function of repeller wheel in the cell wheel precision seeder?

A] Removes the super fluous seeds

B] Ensure uniform deliver of seeds

C] Ensure the seeds to fall down at bottom

D] Provide accurate drilling

106] What is the name of seed drill?

A] Centrifugal seed drill

B] Hand seed drill

C] Pneumatic seed drill

D] Strip till drill

107] What is the type of seed drill?

A] Hand seed drill

B] Centrifugal seed drill

C] Pneumatic seed drill

D] Strip till drill

108] Which is the manually operated seed drill?

A] Centrifugal seed drill

B] Pneumatic seed drill

C] Hand seed drill

D] Cell wheel precision seeder

109] What is the function of seed drills?

A] Digging multiple holes for trans planting

B] Drops seeds uniformly without injurry

C] Grading and levelling of fields

D] Breaking the clods

INDUSTRIAL TRAINING INSTITUTE

Monthly Test-12, Marks- 20, Date:- ______________

(Every Question Carry Two Marks)

1] Which sprayers are operated usually with Internal Combustion engines?

a) Power sprayer

b) Hydraulic sprayer

c) Commercial sprayer

d) Foot sprayer

2] What is the pressure at which Power sprayers are operated?

a) 68-103 kg/cm2

b) 20-55 kg/cm2

c) 106-141 kg/cm2

d) 120-155 kg/cm2

3] What is the rotating speed of an agitator in a power sprayer?

a) 400-500 rev/min

b) 900-1000 rev/min

c) 600-700 rev/min

d) 100-200 rev/min

4] In which nozzle narrow elliptical spray pattern is formed?

a) Hollow cone nozzle

b) Solid cone nozzle

c) Fan type nozzle

d) Nozzle boss

5] The operating pressure of fan nozzle, which is undesirable is _____
a) 1]2 kg/cm2
b) 1]5 kg/cm2
c) 9 kg/cm2
d) 5]9 kg/cm2
6] Which nozzle covers the entire area at small range?
a) Solid cone nozzle
b) Fan nozzle
c) Hollow cone
d) Nozzle tip
7] Which part of power sprayer is used to prevent corrosion?
a) Agitator
b) Strainer
c) Prime mover
d) Tank
8] Which part of power sprayer is used to break the liquid into desired spray and deliver to plants?
a) Boom
b) Nozzle
c) Strainer
d) Pressure gauge
9] What is rate of the spinning disc, attached to the motor, in Ultra low volume sprayer?
a) 4000-9000
b) 1000-3000
c) 750-1000
d) 10000-15000
10] Who invented world's first self-propelled sprayer?
a) Ray Hagie
b) Elon Musk
c) John Deere
d) Rachel Carson

www.ingramcontent.com/pod-product-compliance
Ingram Content Group UK Ltd.
Pitfield, Milton Keynes, MK11 3LW, UK
UKHW021921190726
13853UKWH00002B/780